MW01235055

CUSTOMER SERVICE IS THE BOTTOM LINE

By:
ANDREW CARLSON

Customer Service is the Bottom Line

Customer Service is the Bottom Line by Andrew Carlson

Published by TD Inner Circle

www.andrew-carlson.com

© 2017 Andrew Carlson

help@CornerstoneWriters.com

Cover by Author Your Brand – Doug Crowe.

Hardcover ISBN: 978-0-692-82811-3

Paperback ISBN-13: 978-1640590014

TO: RESTAURANT OWNERS

Never give up.

Never settle for anything less than exceptional.

The industry is better because of you.

Focus on growing.

Focus on adapting.

Focus on impacting.

Focus on thriving.

Focus on prospering.

Anything less is just not worth it...

Cheers!

"The key to excellent customer service isn't always the training, but finding the right people to represent your brand in the first place. Caring is key, so combined with comprehensive training, your employee can succeed in their job which is selling your product. Andrew is the ultimate case of that specific combination and has been an exceptional example of the perfect Customer Service Representative."

- Lindsay Hollister Heffner, Co-Owner of The Pie Hole LA

"I met Andrew at a Chamber of Commerce mixer; that first meeting turned into a 5-hour discussion about service. I was immediately impressed by Andrew's passion for the topic, and we've had many animated discussions since. A great many people give lip service to the importance of service, fewer understand how to walk the talk, and far fewer have the ability to instill that passion in others— Andrew is one of them!"

- Wally Moran, GM of Wood & Vine

"I have had the opportunity to work closely with Andrew, both in a group setting and one-on-one. I have found Andrew to be an exemplary person, proven to have the highest level of integrity and the ability to connect with people in a way that

is compassionate, motivating, and inspiring. As a business person yourself, you know how important your name and reputation are, as do I with mine. And so, I take great care and consideration before personally recommending anyone. If you're reading this, that means you have one of the top trainers, presenters, and public speakers available in the country at your disposal and it would be to your benefit to work with them in any capacity."

-Michael Stevenson, Best-Selling Author, Speaker, and Founder of Transform Destiny & Influence to Profit.

"Andrew Carlson knows exactly what it takes to increase customer service and your bottom line. You have to listen to this guy; he is the real deal!"

-Mike Fritz, International Best-Selling Author, Speaker and Co-Founder of Algorithms for Success.

Table of Contents

YOUR FREE GIFT

Customer Service is the Bottom Line...PERIOD!

I can't tell you how excited I am that this book is in your hands.

The success of your restaurant is contingent on your ability to make every customer that walks through your door love the experience and want to tell others.

I am sure you would agree.

However, you probably also know that if you are going to have great customer service, you are going to have to train your people to love on your customers in a way that they will remember, return and refer you to others.

In this book, I open my playbook and teach what I have learned working with restaurants all over the world; and now it is accessible to you and your team.

Plus, I am going to give you a FREE GIFT that will greatly help you as you train your team to increase customer service so that your bottom line starts to grow.

If you go to *freegiftfromandrew.com,* you can get my all-inclusive training outline that all of your employees should receive so that your customer service increases your bottom line.

As we all know... the real work starts after you read this book and start implementing the ideas in this book at your own restaurant.

Look, training is difficult. Everything is very "situational" and you won't know if you have questions or difficulties until you are actually implementing these ideas.

This is why I would love to keep in touch with every single one of you.

I personally want to hear how things are going.

So, go to *freegiftfromandrew.com* to put in your information and you'll get the training outline instantly as well as some additional surprise information to help shape the culture of your restaurant to increase the bottom line and make every customer feel like family.

CUSTOMER SERVICE IS THE BOTTOM LINE

INTRODUCTION

L ost. Confused. Terrified. These are all of the feelings that I felt on my first day working in restaurants. Now I couldn't think of working anywhere else.

The truth is, like most people, I started working in restaurants to make some money. I wanted to be a server but was turned down a lot due to my little experience in the position. Instead of asking myself why I couldn't get a job, I asked myself what did I have to learn to get a job as a server.

I ended up in working at a Cold Stone Creamery where I just learned that working can be fun. It got busy, but nothing that was too difficult because I was just mixing ice cream and fixings. I wasn't a manager so I didn't have many responsibilities besides making the customer happy.

The thing about Cold Stone Creamery is that you have to sing when you get tipped. Although I was a fan of singing, this got old really quick. What kept it entertaining was that my boss, at the time, allowed us to write our own tip songs to keep us engaged. We were also a bunch of teenagers who only cared about money – we didn't care about customer service. But the owner knew a thing or two on keeping her business profitable and keeping her staff engaged.

Little did I know; this was my first lesson in leadership. Guiding a team of people from all backgrounds towards a common goal.

I applied for a serving job once I turned 17 and told the manager at the time that I wasn't sticking around forever. This job was a means to an end and that end was moving out to Los Angeles but while I was on the floor – I'd be the best employee that they ever hired. Period.

It was a bold statement but that's the goal that I strived for every single day that I stepped into the building. Although that was my personal goal, there wasn't a strong leadership structure within the restaurant. The culture of the restaurant was very different from the AM to the PM. The managers from the AM and the PM had that same mentality which caused many issues for this location.

To be honest, I wasn't really paying attention. I wanted to provide the best experience because I knew that I would get tipped better. There were also those customers that, no matter how hard that you worked, would never tip more than a dollar or two. But they showed up every day to have 6 cups of coffee to chat from midnight-3am.

It wasn't until I started learning about the lives of our customers and talking to them on a regular basis that I realized how important it is for them, to have exceptional service. It wasn't just a night out for some of these people, it was something that they looked forward to once, twice, or even three times a week. This was their escape from whatever they were dealing with at home. For this brief moment in time, they were perfectly content and enjoying their time.

Some people would even want to stay longer so they'd order a dessert or another drink just to carry on the conversation. Unfortunately, I wasn't the best server. I never hit the best beverage percentage and I never had the best guest check average. I simply didn't care about that at the time. I only cared about the money and that's when I started to burn out.

I moved out to Los Angeles, swore off restaurants forever, and started working in the film industry. I loved every minute of the film industry except for the way that people made me feel. I also couldn't make enough money to survive in LA and moved back to Minnesota where I spent another year back at the restaurant saving more money. All of the regulars welcomed me with open arms because I was back which meant that our conversations would continue.

They inspired me to keep trying. To keep pushing myself. To not give up over a silly failure because they knew that I wasn't meant to be there forever.

After I saved up enough money, I moved down to New Orleans and started working steadily on a few movies. On my days off, I would eat at restaurants for every meal. I started studying what made restaurants to special because it was a luxury to go out to eat when I was growing up.

I absolutely fell in love with the southern charm and the way people genuinely greeted me with a smile. These were all family run businesses where their greatest joy was serving amazing food to everyone who walked into the doors. It was their passion – their blood, sweat, and tears went into their restaurant.

They had a vision and that vision was to make their community better because of the food that they serve and the lives that they could touch. Although I only lived in New Orleans for 9 months, those were some of the most meaningful moments of my life. It was during that time when I learned how the regulars at my old restaurant had felt.

I didn't know anyone outside of working on the film because they were 14-18 hour days, 6 days a week. Most people just slept in or partied on their day off – but I went on a search to find the soul of the city since I knew I was only there temporarily. But every server made me feel special and made me feel like I was the only one that mattered while they were talking to me.

That's what I did while working on a film set. I was the one in charge of getting all of the makeup, wardrobe, and executives breakfast every morning. I made sure to make them feel special, every time. There was one person, Greg Cannom (the head special effects makeup artist), that I bonded with on the set of Abraham Lincoln: Vampire Hunter.

He loved pudding cups. So, I would always grab some from lunch to bring to him later on throughout the day when he got a sweet tooth. It was remembering those tiny things that might have seemed silly to me but meant the world to him. He's dealt with a lot of assistants in his day and they are all different but no one had gone out of their way to make sure his experience on set that day was exceptional.

That's what I did with every single person, whether they were a producer, a sound person, or another assistant – like myself.

Once ALVH was ending, Greg had asked me to come out to LA again so I could work with him. I thought about it for a while – worked on one last film, and was treated very poorly. It was in that moment that I knew I had to just take a chance and move back out to Los Angeles.

That's exactly what I did. I worked with Greg for a few months before he had to work on another film in a different country and I just wasn't in the budget for it. I loved my experience working for him but I was missing something – I just didn't know what it was.

I found a job in a reality show production studio working in an entry-level position. I had to make runs to different networks to drop off the edited shows and enjoyed being around a bunch of interesting people from all walks of life.

Once my contract ended, I was once again on the job market. I was struggling to find any kind of steady job because it was a bad time to be unemployed. I would eat one meal per day at restaurants around LA and I wasn't getting the same experience I was getting in New Orleans. I was yearning for that connection with people or an experience that I couldn't forget – but I just wasn't finding that level of service around LA.

I stumbled into the Art's District in Downtown Los Angeles when I saw this bakery across the street. The name alone was enough to spark my interest and I ended up going inside. I was instantly greeted with a smile, ordered a slice of pie and a coffee, and shortly after was asked how my first few bites were.

I was incredibly confused because this was a fast casual business – order at the counter and the food will be brought out to you. It wasn't a full-service restaurant so the employees had to consciously come back to check in to see how things were going. I instantly fell in love with the experience and I had to "check-in" on social media to tell everyone about this place.

That night, I found a job ad posted to be a barista at this location. After multiple interviews with the owners and their managers, I was extended a job offer. This company is called The Pie Hole Los Angeles.

I had the opportunity to get in on the ground floor of a growing company where I have learned so much and have grown personally & professionally. I owe a great deal of my knowledge about leadership, customer service, and even developing an effective training program to the company.

No one was wanting to hire me and the owners took a chance on some kid that turned out to have a strong desire to help them grow & expand. I grew such an interest in training and learning how to be better that I started studying multiple companies. I spent my hard-earned money on my own personal & professional development but The Pie Hole allowed me to test & expand it.

I have helped them open up 5+ of their locations, assisted in creating their training program, and how to keep the company's culture & vision in all of their stores as they expand. It was because of them, that I was able to really focus on how I could impact the industry. I saw how providing exceptional service could touch people, even for a brief period of time.

But I also witnessed first-hand, one of the secrets behind their success – their forward-thinking vision and willingness to admit when they were wrong. They built a team of core individuals who were smarter than they were and people who had a passion for certain aspects of the industry, and they allowed us to grow within those areas. They supported us because they knew that we would be supporting them.

That's what makes that company so special. Without them, I wouldn't have known what I was capable of achieving within the industry. They believed in me when nobody else did and allowed me to grow within their company into a Director of Training position. They didn't say that I was too young – in fact, they let me know how that actually was a benefit.

That's my secret. I am willing to learn, to make mistakes, to admit when I am wrong, and to keep moving forward. I didn't have an ego. I didn't pretend to know it all because I simply didn't know. But the lessons that I have learned to date are invaluable. It's because of them that my mission to bring back the customer experience to restaurants around the world is on fire.

That's why I want to share this book with you. The most important lessons that I have learned are currently in this book. By the time I'm done, I'll have learned a million other lessons. But if you want to be exceptional, then take the time to read each chapter and understand that being exceptional is always a choice. It's a tough path to walk down but no one or no company was ever remembered for being average or mediocre.

To be exceptional, you have to continue to grow and pave your path. I have been fortunate to have learned these lessons early on in my career and the only place to go from here – is up.

Chapter 1:

THE #1 TRAIT THAT DESTROYS A RESTAURANT

> *"Why do so many restaurants close their doors? Because they became addicted to being average and there is no money in being just average."*
>
> - Donald Burns

Imagine creating a plan, fine tuning your plan, and everything just starts falling into place. You bring your business plan to the bank and they give you the loan. You find the PERFECT location and get approved for the space. The build-out happens and people start to take notice!

"A new restaurant is coming! Oh, the name is absolutely perfect. The branding is terrific! This place is going to be wonderful" – you hear bits and pieces as you walk by your own restaurant. The excitement starts to get more intense every day.

You've already started teasing on social media. People are chopping at the bit, waiting impatiently for the day you announce your grand opening.

Press start contacting you about your new place and even the local news stations start reaching out wanting to get bits of you and the place. You put an ad out to start hiring people. Then you take part in the whole hiring process because it's incredibly exciting. This is your moment and everyone is looking at you to lead them into the next phase of the business – being open for business.

"He/She is so lucky to be opening up their own restaurant" you hear amongst your employees who are eager to start their training.

You announce that it's soft opening time. You ask people to make reservations and that you'll even allow walkins. It's almost go time.

Now it's the day of the soft opening to work out the kinks in your operations. Things are flowing smoothly and you're working the room, thanking everyone who came out to the soft opening.

After everyone leaves, you have a pep talk with the employees who are excited for their first few days of service. You provide them with observations and how they can take their service up another level.

It's Grand Opening day. Press is flying through social media. Instagram influencers are swarming to try your place. Photos are being taken. You walk out to the door to welcome everyone to the first "official" day of service and cut the ribbon. People start flooding into your restaurant.

The host starts seating everyone and the line has been created. The reservation list is booked for the whole night! Things are going to be absolutely amazing...

...for now.

*   *   *

There's nothing sexier than opening up a restaurant and being booked for the whole night or having lines out the door with people DYING to get in. But eventually that will fade and reality will set-in that it's actually just the beginning of a difficult path.

You see, people will open up a restaurant because it's been a lifelong dream and they don't have a plan to execute when it doesn't take off right away.

Or maybe it does take off for the first year or two and then suddenly, business just stops coming in as much as it used to - or even at all. That's okay because it's just a slow year for restaurants everywhere, but then time keeps moving forward but your bank account starts getting smaller and smaller. Vendors start calling because you're late on payments and then suddenly, you're faced with the reality that maybe this was a mistake.

The biggest mistake that restaurant owners make is that they don't have a game plan for a rainy day. But that's not what destroys a restaurant.

Not having a plan is a dangerous place to be in but the #1 destroyer of restaurants is not holding onto the belief of the real reason why they opened a restaurant in the first place.

The truth is, when you first got the idea to open a restaurant, you wanted to become the next spot where you can showcase your dream with your community. You planned on being around forever because you were the best and represent a place where the community can come together.

The thing that people don't take into account is that restaurants end up being twice as expensive as they think they are to open and take twice as long to open. This is a huge mistake - it's not just a walk in the park to open the doors.

Most restaurants fall into the average or mediocre category. They put their life savings into a restaurant but don't have enough from the bank to do it exactly the way they want to so they compromise on some aspects of the restaurant. They don't put enough in the ascetics or the atmosphere so they can purchase high tech kitchen equipment. But then when a customer walks into the doors, they're greeted with mediocrity.

But it's your baby! You've put your blood, sweat, and tears into the place just to get it open and to have your dream actualized. It's not fair that people with more money can provide a better atmosphere for guests to dine in.

But you can provide a terrific atmosphere with great staff. But when you go to hire, the pickings are slim. You find people that you think will be great, train them for a couple of days, and then let them serve your guests. Unfortunately, you didn't empower them with enough knowledge or hired quickly because you wanted to get the restaurant open. As time goes on, they just slack off - putting in minimum effort.

So, you think that the way to save your business is going to be your food and solely your food. The food will speak for itself even though the ambiance is just average. It's the best you could do! Truth is, people do not come into a restaurant just for the food.

It's a full experience that you are selling when you open a restaurant so there's absolutely NO chance for your restaurant to survive an extended period of time without a combination of everything listed above.

The key to a successful restaurant is by being the absolute best in your area. This is the foundation of every great restaurant.

Now you're probably thinking, "well, why is it that people with a lot of money and seem to have it all on the outside - have restaurants that fail?"

That is because they don't believe that they are the best.

Let me say that again. They do not truly believe that they are the best. Period.

They may say that they are but the truth lies in their actions of what they do INSIDE of the business. A lot of time, people with money will have money to dump into it but don't put in the effort to actually be the best.

In order to be the best, you need to have the following:

1. The mentality that you are exceptional
2. A solid foundation that you're always working on reinforcing
3. A strong team of people who believe in your vision and goals
4. Systems in place for operational needs
5. Training & on-going coaching/support to improve your team daily
6. Outreach to bring in more customers to fill those tables

The most important one out of all of these is having the belief that you are exceptional. If you don't believe that you are exceptional, you won't do everything in your power to make sure you stay exceptional. You will let the stress of daily operations run your day and you will become addicted with just getting by instead of thriving.

Chapter 2:

IN ORDER TO BE EXCEPTIONAL, YOU MUST HAVE A VISION

> *"You have to have a big vision and take very small steps to get there. You have to be humble as you execute but visionary and gigantic in terms of your aspiration. It's not about grand innovation, it's about a lot of little innovations: every day, every week, every month, making something a little bit better."*
>
> – Jason Calacanis

I am an expert columnist for Foodable TV and one of my biggest articles on the site was on the importance of having a vision. In order to be an exceptional business, you MUST have a vision.

"What do companies like Chili's, Chipotle, Mendocino Farms, and Starbucks all have in common? They all have a vision or a mission that is their sole focus with every decision their company has made.

- Chili's – "Our passion is making people feel special."
- Mendocino Farms – "We sell happy."
- Chipotle – "The business of good food."
- Starbucks – "To inspire and nurture the human spirit — one person, one cup and one neighborhood at a time."

Their visions are greater than just selling food or coffee. They focus on more than just getting customers in the door. A vision is not just about finding that store with high foot traffic. It's not just about making money.

These are companies that have stood the test of time because of their vision. When the going got tough, they didn't throw in the towel. They decided that their vision was greater than the struggles they were experiencing and that they would be doing their communities a disservice by giving up.

But why is having a vision important? I'll refer to my favorite quote to answer this question.

"A goal without a plan is just a wish."

— Antoine de Saint-Exupery

Not having a vision for your brand is like trying to give a tourist in a major city directions, when you yourself have just arrived. It's impossible to succeed besides referring to Google Maps!

It's crucial to have a vision for your company and then for yourself, as the restaurant owner! Your vision is the road map to your success. How can I make such a bold statement by saying if there's no vision, there's only failure? Here are five areas that are influenced by your company's vision.

1. Ownership

Think of your restaurant like a ship. You can just float on the water for an eternity, but wouldn't you want to travel the world instead of just sitting there? Of course you would!

Having a vision will allow you to make smarter decisions from the menu, interior design, hiring and firing, policy creation, and growth and development.

If there are multiple owners, it allows you to find that common ground, in case of they are not able to see eye to eye. It allows you to leave your ego at the door and come together in a way that's for the betterment of the company as a whole — not just as an individual.

2. Employees

Unless you want to greet customers, seat them, take their order, go ring in their order, go cook their order, keep

21

up with their drink requests, and then clear everything, only to go back and wash all of the dishes at the end of the night...chances are you'll be hiring a few employees.

How are they supposed to act or communicate to each other (or to ownership) if they don't see what your goal is as a company? There ends up being no set guidelines and having a free-for-all mentality is a surefire way to lose control.

Have you ever watched "Bar Rescue"? Those bars are on the show because they lost their vision and their staff followed. It's hard to get people to come together for a common goal when there isn't one.

3. Community

A restaurant is only as strong as the community that it roots down into. That's why I think it's silly when restaurants move into a community or neighborhood and they are trying to change everything around it to fit its mold.

That's not how this works in communities. They want to see restaurants come in that already know and understand the vision of the community as a collective.

I'm always impressed by restaurants that come into communities and embrace everything about the surrounding area. They welcome everyone in with open arms and find ways to grow within the community.

If your restaurant has a vision that the community can believe in and can see you walk your talk, you will have raving fans for life.

4. Leader in the Industry

You get to set the new standard for how other restaurants just starting out should look at their own business. The only way industries begin to change is because someone causes a ripple. A restaurant with a vision is that ripple, and it affects the whole industry.

Danny Meyer created a ripple by sharing his vision with his no-tipping policy and why he felt that was an extraordinary decision for his company. Then multiple restaurants followed after.

You get to create change. You get to change the industry and restaurant community for the better. You get the opportunity to set the new standard — if not in the industry — in the community your restaurant is currently in.

5. Passion

At the end of the day, you cannot get through on passion alone. So many more restaurants would be thriving if they were fueled solely on passion. Unfortunately, people lose sight of their goals if it's not clearly defined in the beginning.

It is so easy to fall into the "shiny object" syndrome without a clearly defined vision.

You have to create something that's bigger than yourself and bigger than the restaurant itself. That's why I absolutely love Chili's mission: to make people feel special. Every decision that's going to be made, every customer interaction, or every interaction with their employees will focus on making them feel special.

Companies fail because of multiple reasons, but not having a vision is a surefire way to fail quickly.

Have companies with visions failed? Absolutely and it's not because their vision wasn't big enough. It was because they refused to shift their vision as the communities that they lived in shifted, eating habits shifted, and the customer's that came through the doors have shifted.

If you don't have a vision specific for your restaurant, I challenge you to come up with one and watch how it influences how you do business. I guarantee that it will change everything — for the better."

I want to touch a little deeper on a company that has continued to grow steadily – no matter what the economy or others 'expert analysts' have said – and that company is Chili's.

Like it was stated in my Foodable article, Chili's mission & vision is to make people *feel special*.

They do an amazing job at doing that with every customer, every online interaction, & every potential employee that walks through their doors. What really caught my interest was when I reached out to them via Twitter.

I wasn't a disgruntled customer or someone singing their praise – I was simply inquiring about their training program and what made them, as a company, so successful. It was an open tweet.

Within 30 minutes of tweeting them, they responded back. Here's the conversation below.

Andrew Carlson
@andrew1110

@Chilis - would love to talk to the person in charge of your training programs. Just read a great write up about you in @GQMagazine.

10:18 AM - 12 Jul 2016

Reply to @Chilis @GQMagazine

Chili's Grill & Bar @Chilis · Jul 12
@andrew1110 Thank you for reaching out. A member of our training team will be in touch soon via twitter. Have a great day!

There was a write-up about Chili's and their training program in GQ Magazine. But the article was about a past employee remembering their time at Chili's, the training program, and how much of an impact that it made on his career.

As soon as I read the article, I knew that I just HAD to get to the bottom of what made Chili's such a great company to work for and what made their training program so special.

I had the opportunity to speak with Dom Perry, who is the VP of PeopleWorks at Brinker International (parent company of Chili's). He told me that their secret lies within their vision of where they want to take the company.

Their vision dictates everything that they do as a company, how they treat their employees, how the employees treat their guests, and how the overall experience is elevated all because of a simple vision of the company.

Let's break it down even further.

First, it starts with their people. They don't just hire some random 'Joe Schmoe' or 'Suzie Somebody' off of the street. They take their time to find the right personality to fit their brand and vision.

As Dom put it, they empower their managers to look for people that have the *hospitality gene*. It's okay if they don't have every skill needed to fulfill the position because skills can be taught. What cannot be taught is personality and the act of caring for people.

They look for someone who is going to understand what hospitality truly means and will take their time to make sure the guests feel special.

In order for the employees to be empowered to make every guest feel special, Brinker International makes every single employee feel special. The way they do this is simple.

They turn someone from someone who was hired and turn them into "Chili Heads" by sharing the culture, the love of the brand, and the purpose behind it – their heritage.

You see, someone cannot fall in love with someone (or a brand) without knowing its past and the story behind what makes them who they are today. You don't fall in love with a romantic partner until you get to know them more and the same goes for your employees.

[We will go into depth more of how to create these kinds of power-house teams that will take your brand to the next level in a later chapter.]

It was through this conversation that I got to ask Dom the biggest question that I have had and was one of the reasons that sparked the title of this book. I asked him, "do you think service directly impacts the bottom line? If so, how?"

That's when I heard him smile and without missing a beat, he said, "Absolutely."

It may seem like a no brainer to most people, but they are at the level where they have actual data that proves this statement. It's just like with Starbucks – they can predict customer behavior on a much larger scale than smaller businesses can because they have such large databases to back up their findings.

They continue to strive for exceptional and they know that they are – every single day with every single interaction. They know that *Customer Service is the Bottom Line.*

Why is customer service the bottom line?

I truly believe that customer service is the bottom line simply because you can directly impact your sales & customer experience through the customer service you provide – instantly.

It's not like investing in marketing services to wait for results and then trying to measure based on speculation, business analytics, & data provided to you from the marketing companies.

By providing exceptional service & creating a fun workplace environment that empowers their employees to BE exceptional – you can directly impact your bottom line right away.

Chili's focuses on making people feel special. But what does that mean to the employee and how can you TRAIN someone to be exceptional when everyone's definition of exceptional may be different?

Dom Perry says it boils down to 2 things.

1. Passion
2. Purpose

When you train someone with passion and a purpose, they will then convey the excitement from the trainer and the other employees within the company. It doesn't matter if they're a dishwasher, bus person, server, chef, line cook, management, executives, etc.

Everyone must have the same passion for the company and that starts with the leadership of the company.

Chili's PURPOSE is serving more than just food. It's creating an experience that is unlike any other. They want every single person who walks into the door to feel so special, that they will become a raving, loyal fan for life.

Their purpose isn't just based on what they sell. It's what they stand for as a company and the LIFE that they want their employees to live.

It's a passion of Chili's for their employees to create the *best life* that they possibly can because they know it's vital to the success of the business. A manager cannot be as efficient or successful in leading a team if they do not have an exceptional life outside of work.

Their employees cannot bring their vision to life is they do not have success in these areas of life:

Well-Being

If your team isn't staying healthy and maintaining a healthy lifestyle, it will cause them to create stress which will lead to sickness and needing time off. If they continue to achieve a healthy living, they will have more energy and be more productive during work hours.

Social

Everyone needs a social life. Everyone needs time to disconnect and Chili's understands that efficiency starts to diminish when someone feels trapped within their job. When someone has a social life, they are able to de-stress and come back the following day feeling rejuvenated having been around friends & family.

Personal

Having personal time is incredibly important to every single people. When people don't have time for their personal time, they will get cranky and can end up with a short fuse. I've seen this happen personally and when things get stressful on the floor due to an increase in volume, not having personal time will cause unnecessary stress and lead to poor morale for the team.

Career

People need to know that their career is going somewhere. Nothing will kill morale faster than realizing you're working at a dead-end job. Even if you are the most appreciative owner in the world, not having upward mobility in a career path will cause those people to lose their passion that they have for the company and the industry.

Finances

If your employees are constantly worrying about their finances, they won't be able to focus on what matters – selling personal experiences with the customers. When you pay your employees well, they will be able to spend more time focusing on doing better within the business.

*   *   *

Because when you, as the employee, have a well-rounded life – you have the ability to change lives through making people *feel special.*

At the end of the day, Chili's wants you to look through its "corporate" infrastructure and see it as a small, growing company that has the ability to connect with their customers on a deeper level. That's one of their biggest reasons for their steady growth.

Their framework is that it's up to you and your perception of what YOU, as the employee, think would impact every customer. They ask themselves, "How can I make that person *feel special*, even after just meeting them for the very first time?" throughout every shift.

Although there is structure, they have the freedom to create that experience for every customer with the brand's vision to assist in every decision that's being made.

That's what makes Chili's such a strong company within the industry. They never forget where they came from but they are always looking toward the future and how they can make a bigger impact in their communities.

The secret isn't in creating a concept that works – it's creating a brand that has something to say and has a plan to do it. That's the true path to success and Chili's does it very well.

It's what has kept them around for 40 years with continual growth through economic hardships and other factors.

They strive to be exceptional every step of the way and believe that they are the best. Period.

Chapter 3:

GET IT RIGHT 100% OF THE TIME

> *"Exceptional customer service starts at the top. If your senior people don't exude it, even your strongest links down the chain will become infected."*
>
> – Andrew Carlson

G rowing up, my mother always cooked dinner for me. It was a rare occurrence to actually get to go out to eat, so everything always fell onto the decision of "what are you in the mood to eat".

Now, people spend anywhere from 5-45 minutes looking through Yelp and Trip Advisor (mainly Yelp though, let's be honest) to figure out where they want to eat.

I remember sifting through Yelp trying to figure out what I was in the mood to eat. (One of life's hardest & most decisions of my generation.) 3 stars, 4 stars, 5 stars – what does it all mean!?

First impressions are everything.

Everyone knows this to be true because as an employer, we judge people every single day.

What is the first thing that you do when you start interviewing people? You screen them by a piece of paper. If they are qualified or meet your standards to call them in for an interview, you will give them the opportunity to impress you.

What are you looking for in this potential employee? Well, that doesn't matter as much as the sole reason why you called them in. You are looking to see if they can give you an exceptional first impression.

That's exactly what the customers that come into your restaurant are looking at. The world has become more money conscious than ever before because it's their hard-earned money that they are spending. They want to have an exceptional experience if they are going to be giving money to your business.

At the end of the day, that's what they're looking for and I know that you already know that.

But is it being done? Is the experience that you're providing them an exceptional experience? That is the question that I want you to ask yourself every single day.

Why? Why should you care that every single customer's experience is an exceptional one?

Because you are in the restaurant industry. You're in the service industry. You're in the industry to serve people; to make them FEEL like they are the only ones in the room. Even if you have a packed dining room and the kitchen is 15+ tickets deep with a 60-minute ticket time - you have to make them feel like the most important people in the room.

What if you don't?

What if your employee or your whole team drops the ball?

It's bound to happen so I'm not going to pretend that it doesn't. Even Danny Meyer's restaurant drops the ball every once in a while. The thing that separates the exceptional experiences from the mediocre ones are when the team steps up to the occasion.

I'm never going to say that every experience needs to be perfect. That's the goal but just like in life, there is no such thing as perfection. There's providing an exceptional experience or there is something to be learned and adjusted within your leadership if the experience falls short.

That's the golden nugget that everyone searches for.

People desire to go into a restaurant and expect perfection. The food is perfect, the drinks are out of this world, the service is top quality, and they leave incredibly happy.

But people are incredibly understanding at their very core. We are all humans and we all have times in our life we just want to throw in the towel so I strongly believe in open communication.

35

In reality though, the majority of customers who have poor experiences will not even let a manager know.

It is said that 96% of unhappy customers don't complain but 91% of those will simply leave and *never come back.* *

(#1 Source: 1Financial Training Services)

This is why it is critical to adopt the mindset that you MUST get it right 100% of the time. Every day, your employees must go in ready to be the beacon of excellence. This stems from ownership and trickles down so if the ownership doesn't start adopting this quality, it will not spread through the company.

Whenever anything goes wrong, you must always look within to figure out the issues.

The customer was upset?

How was this handled?

Was it handled at all?

If it was handled, how did the employee handle it?

Did they get the manager?

What did the manager do in order to win the customer over to maintain that level of excellence and to create an exceptional experience for every customer?

You see, customers are not looking for everything to be perfect. They're looking for an exceptional experience.

Whether that experience has some hiccups throughout it or if it's seamless - it doesn't matter. As long as you are aiming for excellence in every little thing that you do, you will win over the customer every single time.

There are very few industries that rely solely on customer service and the restaurant industry is one of those industries. It doesn't matter how amazing the food is, if the service is mediocre, then the whole experience is valued as a mediocre experience and you will not have returning customers.

There are so many variables within the restaurant industry that you have going against you. Whether you're the owner, the manager, or the hourly employee - just because you have an exceptional year doesn't mean that you can slack it off.

It doesn't mean that your doors will remain open forever. Restaurants close for all kinds of reasons and it's your responsibility to do everything that you can to keep those doors open.

"You get it right 100% of the time."

You put in the effort to make it work.

As the owner, you get it right 100% of the time when it comes to your employees and your team.

As the manager, you get it right 100% of the time to your team, the ownership, and the customers.

As the hourly employee that is busting their ass, you get it right 100% of the time. That's why you get a paycheck. Your paycheck is given to you in a timely manner for a "job well done". If you aren't performing, your employer has every right to discipline you to let you know where you stand with the company or simply to let you go.

That's the beauty of this industry.

You either want to be in it or you don't. Those that don't want to be in it end up weeding themselves out.

But when you adopt the mentality of getting it right 100% of the time, you are adopting greatness.

Greatness is defined as "exceptionally high quality" in the Merriam-Webster Dictionary.

That is what you must strive for to be successful in this industry. As a chef, server, host, manager, trainer, owner, etc. If you are not striving for greatness in everything that you do, then you are bound to fail.

You must get it right 100% of the time.

Now, how can you get your employees to adopt a mindset when they're only in their job for their paycheck?

You MUST make it personal to them.

That's where your training program comes in.

You cannot get people to buy-in to your vision and mission in your community when you do not invest in your employees.

Most restaurants struggle with hiring the right people because they only interview when they need to find people. If you are constantly interviewing, you have a constant pool of people to choose from. When you find those needles in the haystack, you make room for them on your schedule and get them training.

They will be the people you want as the face of your company - not the people that are only there for the paycheck or the ones who aren't performing to your standards.

Does your company even have a training program?

I've seen many restaurants who train their new employees by simply throwing them in and expecting them to swim. Not only are they expected to swim, but they are also expected to know every policy and procedure without being properly walked through it.

That is all foundational work.

Your foundation consists of your core values as a company, your mission, and your training program.

Your values are what you want people to know about your company. What does your company stand for in their community? That's vital information to know. If you don't know what your company stands for then what's the point of having a company? Take a stand and create value in the community that you serve!

Your mission statement is what can your employees hold on to?

I recently spoke with Dom Perry over at Chili's and their mission is to make people feel special.

That's a very personal mission statement and is something that every one of their employees can relate to. Every person walks into their shift trying to figure out how they can make every single person they interact with, feel special TODAY. It doesn't matter that they were in last week or that they come in every Monday - how can YOU make them FEEL special while they're in your 4 walls?

Lastly, your training program. The majority of training programs fail because they are training people to be status quo employees without supervision.

I've seen this countless times and it hurts me every time that I talk to restaurant owners who either a. Don't have a training program or b. The end result of their training program is to be able to get them on the schedule without being supervised.

It's time to change the way you see your employee training.

We're talking about getting it right 100% of the time. Not just some of the time. Not the majority of the time. ONE HUNDRED PERCENT OF THE TIME.

In order to achieve something so great, you must shift the way you think about your training program.

You must realize that your company is more valuable than just getting someone onto the schedule.

Adopt the mentality that your restaurant is the best restaurant that every potential employee will ever work at. We're talking about getting it right 100% of the time. If you don't believe your restaurant will be the best place to work at, you cannot say you are getting it right 100% of the time!

It's that simple.

Your training must be so exceptional, that your employees are treating it like an audition.

By the end of their training, you are evaluating (whether that's at ownership level or management level) if the employees in training are the exception. If they are simply getting by, it's more cost effective to let them go than it is to keep them on.

Why?

They will only do the bare minimum.

You must find the employees that will go above and beyond the status quo. You must be searching for excellence and if they don't reach the level of excellence that you view as your STANDARD, then they sure as hell don't have any right to be working at your restaurant or company.

Make it black and white.

At the end of the day, this is business. There should be zero emotions in the decision-making process of your business.

The trainee is either qualified and has shown excellence throughout the training program or they don't work for you. It doesn't make them bad people; it just means that they cannot work for your company.

Your training program is essential to your success. Whether you want to believe it or not.

I asked the Dom Perry at Chili's (who has been around for over 40 years) what they look for in terms of potential employees that apply to their stores. The #1 thing that they said was their attitude. You cannot train someone to have a positive outlook on life. You cannot train someone to remain positive throughout a rush and keep a smile on their face. No matter how bad you want to be able to, that is just something that cannot be trained.

You can train someone on hard skills like carrying a tray or handling tough situations when customers get upset but you cannot train HOW someone treats another person. That is a personal quality that people either have or they don't.

Chili's builds on their customer service throughout their training program and that's how you must look at your training program.

Throughout the training, the trainer must ask themselves "does this person have the qualities that we are looking for?"

If they are, then they move onto the schedule. If they don't, that's okay! Remember, it doesn't make them bad people, it just means that they cannot work for your company because your standards are that your employees get it right 100% of the time.

The truth is that customer service is the bottom line. The way your employees treat your customers and the experience that they provide every single person has everything to do with your bottom line.

Are you struggling? Maybe it's time to take a look at your employees and how they're treating your guests. Every restaurant that I've gone in to that is struggling needs to improve their employees' performance.

The fastest way to boost your sales is to have your team provide the customers with an exceptional experience. I've seen first-hand that the better the experience, the more money that the customer will spend within your establishment. It doesn't matter if you are a fast-casual concept, casual dining, or even a fine dining establishment.

The experience that your team provides has a direct correlation to your bottom line.

How can you implement the rule of getting it right 100% of the time?

1. Get your leadership team on board
2. Communicate your new vision with your management team
3. Re-visit how people are being trained
4. Daily coaching to remind people of achieving excellence
5. Holding people accountable for not reaching your standards

You cannot flip a switch and things will magically be better. That's not how this works.

If an airplane is off target by 1%, they will be completely off course by the time they think they should be reaching their destination.

That's why you picked up this book. You've gone off course and you're looking at how to improve your bottom line. Training and customer service are two of the biggest things that you have control over.

You cannot convince someone that they like something if their taste buds don't agree with them. What you can convince someone of is the experience that you provided was exceptional. That's getting it right 100% of the time.

Your managers must be holding your teams accountable to ensure that they are getting it right 100% of the time. They must be touching every table that comes into the restaurant and check up on how their team is doing.

Remember that 91% of the time, people won't let anyone know if they had a poor experience. But as the manager, if you show up at their table and ask this one question, you will know exactly what you have to do to give that customer an exceptional experience.

That question is; "what could we have done, that would have made your experience a little better?"

Most managers will come around and ask if everything is okay. The issue with that is they are nodding their head while they're asking it so of course, the customer will feel compelled to say everything is okay!

But when you pose an open-ended question that gets them to think, they are more willing to let you know where the holes are in your restaurant to be able to achieve the status of getting it right 100% of the time.

It all boils down to this one question:

What intention do you have?

With every decision that you make in your business, what is your intention for everything that you do? Then *how* will you make it happen?

*   *   *

I have to give credit to the ownership of The Pie Hole LA for this because this is something that they focused on every single day within their company. This was ingrained into my brain as an entry-level employee, middle management, and even their Director of Training.

Everything that we did has a purpose. Everything that we said, had a purpose. Everything was incredibly intentional. A lot of what I learned, I learned through listening to Lindsay, Matt, & Sean – as individuals and as a team. They were incredible mentors to me and have impacted how I communicate with others.

Chapter 4:

WHEN IT COMES TO LEADERSHIP - LOOK WITHIN, NOT OUTWARDS

> *"Leadership is not an expertise. Leadership is constant education."*
>
> – Simon Sinek

I remember walking into a shift at a restaurant I worked with and the place was just BOOMING. The line was out the door, the waitlist was over 90 minutes to get a table, the host stand is in a frenzy, the kitchen staff were focused, and the servers were all busting their ass to get out of the weeds.

All of a sudden, the manager comes storming out of the office. I just hear a stern voice call at me; "Andrew, in my office, NOW!"

I was mortified. This was my first job as a server. What did I already do to screw this up?!

Now, this was the day before Yelp and reviews were even a thing. But apparently, someone complained about me from a previous night via email because I didn't fill their water glass one more time before they left for the night. I just gave them the bill and disappeared, the email said.

The manager went on and on about how important it was to ensure that every guest felt catered to, even after the bill has been paid. As long as they were sitting there, they were still my responsibility until they were no longer there.

But I was not trained that way. I didn't want to start a heated argument while the floor was crazy so I just asked to get out on the floor to help everything. After a huff and puff, he agreed that it's important to get through the rush.

Once the rush was over, we continued our one-sided conversation about the importance of being a server. I just nodded but the whole time, I was thinking, shouldn't he had been out in the dining room following up with customers during that rush? Why did he lock himself in the office while we were all out here busting our ass? It didn't make any sense.

But later on, in my career, I learned that he was simply my boss. He wasn't a leader. Bosses point blame. Leaders take the blame and learn how to improve their operations moving forward.

Truth is, there are not a lot of people out there that are willing to look within themselves to fix the problems that they're experiencing in their lives and the same goes for business owners.

It doesn't matter what's wrong in their company, they are always just looking for someone or something to blame. You hear it all of the time when restaurants try social media marketing for the first time.

I have heard every excuse in the book to write off why something isn't working.

"I don't have the time to be posting on social media - I have a business to run!"

"I tried it a couple times but I didn't see the ROI of running ads. If I wanted to burn through money, then I'd legitimately throw money onto the stove and watch it burn. At least it would be satisfying to watch it burn..."

The list is endless and it's the same thing whenever something is wrong within the organization.

Before you throw this book down in disgust that I would say such a thing, just hear me out for a few pages.

In the last chapter, we discussed the importance of getting it right 100% of the time. Well, what happens when you don't get it right 100% of the time? What happens when your manager screws up?

You look up.

Did you train this person enough to ensure that they wouldn't make those mistakes? If you did, can you prove it?

Do you have written proof that they signed off on every aspect of the job that you require them to do?

Is their signature or initials sitting next to the task that they messed up on?

If you have written proof that they verified they would be able to perform a certain task but they fell short, then you have every right to allow the consequences to lie where they may. But what if you don't?

Sure, you might have mentioned it but it was never verified that they could perform the position to your standards.

This is what I was talking about when I talked about getting it right 100% of the time. It's not just about getting it right with the customers. Yes, they are a crucial part of your business and you wouldn't be able to survive without your customers. That's a given.

But when anyone in your organization fails; whether it's an entry-level employee, to your middle management, even to your senior officers or C-level executives - you MUST look up through the organization to see why you are failing.

This is the only way that you will be able to overcome any obstacle that comes your way because this is the team mentality. This is having the self-awareness to know that if anyone within your team fails, everyone gets the opportunity to learn from it.

I remember one time that I was sitting at home when my phone rang. The owner of the cafe that I was managing was calling me and as soon as I answered, I instantly knew this wasn't a "how are you doing" conversation. His anger just spewed through the phone into my ear.

Apparently, one of my managers had taken it upon himself to defrost a piece of equipment (a fridge) by taking a screwdriver and chipping away at the ice that was in the back.

They finished the night up and closed down the store. I get a phone call the next morning from my morning manager and he said that it smelled funny in the restaurant. I had him call the maintenance guy just to make sure that nothing was out of the ordinary in the restaurant. I was taking the day off so I just brushed it off thinking that it would be handled since he was basically my assistant manager.

15 minutes later, I got the phone call from the owner who was incredibly upset.

Apparently, he had punctured the free-on tube and it was spewing out gas all night long.

$5,000+ in damages. Ouch.

But what impressed me was once it was handled, we had a meeting to figure out how this incident could have happened. How could someone just take it upon themselves to just do something without confirming with the manager that hacking away with a screwdriver at the ice was the proper procedure?

We looked up at ourselves and learned that we never trained them on how to handle a situation where there was ice that started forming on the back of the fridge. I mean, nowhere in any of the training materials was how to defrost a fridge that kept a keg inside!

That brings up 2 very distinct issues within the company.

The first one was that we just didn't train them properly on the new piece of equipment. We didn't expect it to freeze over as we just rolled this out only 2 weeks before.

The second issue within the organization was that we had allowed this location to operate with a culture of just figuring it out as time goes on. There was no real structure and it was definitely a wakeup call when the incident happened.

That is why I wholeheartedly believe that in order to achieve any level of success in the restaurant industry, whenever there are issues within the company (no matter the size), we must always look within to find the issues.

Again, I'm not saying that the CEO or the owner of the company is always to blame. That is so far from the truth.

But just as Sandra Bullock in Eat, Pray, Love had to go find herself to figure out what she wanted out of life - we must also look within ourselves - look within the organization to figure out how we can solve these issues.

Many restaurants are merely existing without tackling their issues head on. They will look to place the blame on someone, something, or anything because the owners are feeling out of control.

That's why they react poorly to Jon Taffer when he goes into the bars and tells them what they're doing wrong with their business.

Listen, this isn't an easy thing to digest. I understand that.

As the owner or the manager, it's not always going to be your fault. But leadership is about digesting the issue and coming up with solutions to allow your company to move forward and learn from your past.

When you decided to open the restaurant, or manage a restaurant, you were putting that burden on your shoulders and saying "let me help you come up with solutions, together. We're all in this together."

And that is the exact way that you need to start approaching every issue within your company.

Are you constantly hiring people that just aren't the right fit?

Why are you frustrated with your management team? What is it that they're failing to do? What is it that you're failing to do if they're failing?

It's not just about one person being at fault.

Either the company grows together or it learns together but it definitely cannot run with 1 person doing everything. That's why we hire a team of people to help us run the restaurant.

There's an African Proverb that says; *"If you want to go fast, go alone. If you want to go far, go together."*

In order to go far and achieve extraordinary results, you absolutely have to move forward together - as a team.

If you're constantly blaming others within your organization when things go wrong - that's not moving forward together. You're singling someone out and slapping them on the wrist.

When you single someone out, you're breaking a link on your chain.

Again, it could be over something incredibly stupid. It could have been over the employee being tired and they just handled a situation poorly.

But instead of slapping them on the wrist and putting your company morale in jeopardy, consider looking within the organization.

Did you equip your employees with the knowledge and tools to handle any situation, no matter how they felt before coming onto their shift? Did you have a meeting to have them shake it off and refocus their goals for that day in particular?

If not, that's a leadership mistake.

Always, always, always look up. Look within your organization. How are you, as a leader to your employees and as a leader in your industry, going to make this the best experience for your guests?

If I'm going to be honest, it's not by routine. You have to shake up your team every single day. As a manager, as an owner, or even as another entry level employee - your position does not prevent you from taking a moment to build your team up.

Anyone who tries to tell you otherwise shouldn't be working within your organization anyway because that's not a team mentality.

Everything that you do starts at the top. Every failure should be felt at the top and every success should be spread around equally. Because without your team, you don't have a company.

Let them take ownership of their mistakes and let this be a learning experience for the organization. You're either succeeding together or you're learning together.

I was once told that it's lonely at the top. Being a leader is lonely because not a lot of people will truly understand what you're going through or what you're struggling with. But I don't believe that to be true.

It's only lonely at the top when you don't surround yourself around extraordinary people.

It's only lonely at the top when you don't have a support system in place of other people in similar positions as you.

It's only lonely at the top because YOU make it lonely at the top. YOU are the sole reason why you are lonely at the top. It's that simple.

It should never be lonely at the top of your organization because you should be focused on growing people and grooming them to be exceptional leaders.

Why?

Your organization is only as good as the team that you assemble.

When you have an exceptional team, your company will do exceptional things.

When you are lonely at the top, that means that you ran a fear based company. Your employees are so afraid to fail that when they do fail, they are terrified to communicate that failure to you. Then you get upset because your employees do not communicate their mistakes with you and you had to figure out after the fact that they actually failed.

Leading a team from a state of fear is a weak style of leadership.

Actually, I wouldn't even call that leadership.

I call it manipulative and controlling.

You cannot keep people happy and satisfied in an organization when they feel like they are walking on eggshells on a daily basis.

With so many moving parts within a restaurant, it's hard not to get upset when things go wrong. All we want to do is scream and tell them that if they cannot handle this level of intensity, maybe they should find another line of work.

But you cannot assume that everyone is equipped with the right tools to handle every situation. Just because someone was a manager at one company doesn't mean they fully understand the position within your organization. It's your job to teach them and to coach them into excellence based off of your standards.

I want to let you in on a secret of the industry. Your employees will treat your customers as well as they are being treated within your organization.

Richard Branson says that his employees always come first because they are the front line of defense within his organization. He has to focus on leading his business and his employees are the ones who have to deal with the customers. When you empower your employees, and treat them with respect, they will respond by treating every customer with respect.

They will go to battle for you and they will defend your honor every step of the way.

Instead of just having employees, you need to create brand ambassadors. With the amount of competition that's out there, not only for your customers, but your employees as well, it's vital to treat everyone with the same amount of respect as you would anyone else within the organization.

Customer service is the bottom line but you cannot grow your bottom line with mediocre employees. You cannot achieve exceptional things with a mediocre mindset. And you most certainly cannot have exceptional customer service by being a mediocre leader for your organization.

Mediocrity is a poison that will infect your business quicker than anything else. Always push yourself and your company to be exceptional. No excuses.

Chapter 5:

THE KEY DIFFERENCES BETWEEN CUSTOMER SERVICE & EXPERIENTIAL SERVICE

"Smart companies have figured out the focus must be on the customer."

– Shep Hyken

Everything in the restaurant industry boils down to service. Your business will live and die by the service that you provide - whether you would like to believe that or not.

A Harvard University study showed the revenue difference between a restaurant with 3 stars and a restaurant with 5 stars on Yelp. The restaurant with 5 stars earned 18% more in revenue than the restaurant with only 3 stars.

Ex: If your restaurant is bringing in $1 million in revenue but then drop down to a 3-star rating, you are losing at least $180,000 in sales!

The key to receiving higher ratings on Yelp boils down to your service.

Why is that?

People understand that taste is very subjective. You either like it or you don't.

You can also ask anyone that goes to a restaurant - they will forgive a restaurant for having mediocre food with exceptional service but they will not forgive a restaurant for having exceptional food but mediocre service.

Service is the secret to the Restaurant Industry that's always hidden in plain sight.

As a manager, one of your responsibilities is growing the sales of your restaurant. You study the numbers, keep costs down, and ensure your team is running efficiently while maintaining guest satisfaction.

But there are 2 issues that jump out instantly.

1. Maintaining Guest Satisfaction
2. Growing Sales

Let's focus on the first issue right away and this one is very important. What happens when you only maintain guest satisfaction?

Sure, you keep your regular customers happy. So, what's the issue then?

You are simply MAINTAINING their satisfaction. There's no going above and beyond. There's no WOW factor. There's no magic to their visit to your establishment.

On top of everything - food costs keep rising [due to many factors] but the customers aren't fully educated on the mathematics of restaurant math. How do I know? I tried explaining it to many customers when I was a server and they simply didn't care. That's when I realized that I had to shift my approach.

Why do sales people have sales goals every single month? Because that is the absolute MINIMUM they must achieve to continue working for that company.

But wouldn't the company to staff their team up with people that are constantly exceeding those minimum sales goals? Absolutely!

It's the same thing in the restaurant world.

Society is at a place where we are so focused on instant gratification. Once their food is delivered, it instantly has to be uploaded to Instagram, Snapchat, or any other social media platforms before even digging in because they want their friends to EXPERIENCE what they are experiencing.

61

They want that instant gratification of "oh I wish I was there" and it gives an ego boost to the person going through that current experience.

That is what it boils down to - an experience.

When you maintain standards, you are not providing an experience that the customer wants to be a part of. They want to be treated like royalty because they are spending their hard-earned money on a meal they want to enjoy.

It's not just the meal though - they are coming to experience your restaurant with their friends, family, special interest, etc.

People are coming to escape their routine and create a memory that they can look back on. Whether that's sharing a special occasion, closing on a business deal, getting together for happy hour with co-workers, or they're just too lazy to cook and want to have a warm meal prepared so they don't have to think about what to make.

Now that you are understanding where the customer is coming from - that they want an EXPERIENCE - it's going to be so much easier for you to grow your sales.

One of the quickest ways to boost your bottom line is to focus on your 4-walls marketing. Focus on marketing to your current customer base that's already inside of your restaurant. You don't have to do the chasing; you don't have to do the prospecting - their butts are already in the seats!

The heavy lifting is already done.

I worked in both full service and fast casual concepts so I understand that even though they are completely different - the experiential formula is still the same.

Perceived Enjoyment + Experience = More Money Spent

When customers are enjoying their time within your restaurant, they're enjoying the experience that they've had - they will spend more money.

Regardless if they want to spend more money, they will want to continue the experience, so they'll get that extra glass of wine or that dessert that they turned down when they were first asked if they wanted anything else.

A lot of restaurants solely focus on turning tables - getting them in and out so they can be replaced with another group of people who will spend money at the restaurant. That was the fast food concept for a very long time - it was about volume and not the service provided.

Fast food got its start because people were working long hours and to save time, they would hit a fast food place to eat while they were on their way home so they could focus on what matters the most - their family or friends. Eventually, people started becoming more aware of what goes into their food so they started shying away from fast food restaurants.

If they were going to spend their money, it was going to be on something they enjoyed. Period.

Which is why fast casual concepts were increasing in popularity. It was great for people crunched for time and didn't want to be at the mercy of how quick the server was. They could order their food on their time, eat on their time, and not be "bothered" while they were there.

Now, fast casual concepts have had to start adapting again as casual dining started increasing in popularity all over again.

A company that does this well is one that I worked for, called The Pie Hole LA. It was a fast-casual concept but we trained everyone to think of it like a full-service restaurant.

Instead of having everything begin and end at the counter, they taught me the importance of checking in with every single customer and ensuring that their having an enjoyable experience.

The experience at a Pie Hole is different than any other restaurant out there. It's like walking into a little Narnia.

It's a growing cafe style concept of sweet & savory pies and coffee. So, when the customers walked in, they were already blown away so they set expectations high from a brand standpoint.

When you set high standards, your staff must also achieve those standards otherwise the experience will fall flat.

To ensure that the customers were getting the best experience of their life (whether it was their first time or millionth visit), the employee at the customer would walk them through any questions that they had. They would also engage with them on a deeper level of how they heard about the company.

Then once the food was running out, the customer was given the low down of where they could find condiments and asked if they needed anything else. If the customer asked for anything, even if it was a glass of water (even though the water pitcher was self-service by the register), the expo person would run them back out a glass of water.

The team was never done checking in with the customers until they had left.

But everything was solely focused on creating an exceptional experience, that once in a lifetime feeling of feeling like the most important person in the room.

That's how we need to approach every customer interaction moving forward because the truth is, the customer expectations are only going to get higher and higher as time goes on.

The 2nd issue that we were talking about was growing sales. When managers are told to focus on growing their sales, they instantly think that they have to run a social media campaign or that they have to do some kind of outward marketing to get new customers in the restaurant to boost their bottom line.

That's simply not a healthy way of thinking about your bottom line because it's going to take an investment to get new customers into your restaurant. It's expensive to find new customers and turn them into raving fans.

Which is why it's crucial to have a loyalty or rewards program associated with your restaurant.

You want a platform that you can reach out to your current customer base but you won't have a loyal fan base if you cannot provide an experience that they remember and rave about for days, weeks, months, or even years. The bigger impact that you can make on someone, the better opportunity you have for them to come back again and again.

Word of mouth is still one of the most powerful marketing tactics because of social media - everyone is connected to so many more people than ever before.

Which can also backfire on you because most people will voice when they are dissatisfied with their experience but most people that have a great experience will remain silent. They'll come back to your establishment but the majority won't voice their opinion.

But the customers with exceptional, VIP treatment experiences, will shout your name to the sky in excitement over the way that you made them feel.

Maya Angelou said it best when she said that *"at the end of the day, people won't remember what you said but they remember how you made them feel"* and that rings true in the restaurant world as well.

Experiences insight feelings within people - touch them on an emotional level that most restaurants aren't willing to achieve - and you'll be in business forever.

Chapter 6:

CUSTOMER SERVICE ISN'T A DEPARTMENT, IT'S YOUR BRAND'S LIFESTYLE

> *"You'll never have a product or price advantage again. They can be easily duplicated, but a strong customer service culture can't be copied."*
>
> – Jerry Fritz

I have spent a lot of time on the phone with technical support for various POS systems and the biggest pet peeve of mine is that they have absolutely no concept of customer service.

Their only focus is on fixing the tech issue that's there and then moving onto the next person with the next issue. This is why many people call into them so frustrated because POS systems are basically like operating a spaceship.

But what if companies took more time to train every single employee of theirs on the 'people skills' necessary to ensure that every customer had an exceptional experience? Do you think that would make a huge difference on company ratings? I do! Especially in the tech world.

How does this relate to the restaurant industry though?

Well, I've seen many restaurants completely fail when it comes to their people skills – whether it's online through a customer review/complaint or the bus people absolutely ignoring someone who's trying to ask them a question.

I remember eating at a restaurant and all of a sudden, my server disappeared. I waited for 10-15 minutes after my meal for the check and the server was nowhere to be found. I tried flagging down the bus boy who was wiping down a table a few tables down from me.

The issue was he just completely ignored me. He heard me because he looked over at me but then just continued doing what he was doing and went into the back.

I couldn't believe it.

Then I asked another server and he said, "Oh, he took his break. He should be back in 15 minutes or so."

The server knew I was irritated and asked if I needed anything. I just asked for the check and if this was normal.

He said that this server does have a habit of just leaving tables waiting until he gets back from his breaks.

I also asked if the bus boy had any training on how to handle customers and he said that the manager that runs this place doesn't let the people that bus tables interact with the customers because they aren't as knowledgeable as another server.

This absolutely blew my mind. This restaurant was not empowering their employees to help out a customer in need. If there was a sign posted on every table that said: "Please do not ask the bus people any questions as they are not empowered to know anything about the business besides their job" – then maybe, I would have a different reaction but I found this absolutely astonishing.

Customer service or the customer experience needs to be a lifestyle that the restaurant embodies – it shouldn't just be left up to certain people that engage with the customers on a daily basis.

The truth is, anyone that works in your company, has the potential to interact with anyone at the restaurant.

Here's the real kicker – they even have the potential to interact with anyone OUTSIDE of your restaurant as well.

That's when all of the truth comes out anyway.

I can't tell you how many times I left work at The Pie Hole and decided to grab a few things from the grocery store before getting home. People would see my shirt and say "Oh my – I absolutely LOVE The Pie Hole! You are so lucky to work there…"

They would just rave about the food, the service, and everything about the company.

Now, this could have gone one of two ways.

The first way would have been if the company didn't empower me to be such a strong brand ambassador, I could have just rolled my eyes and walked away or said something to stop the conversation.

In that moment, though, that person would have realized that the company either didn't hire the right people or don't care enough about their employees to create a fun work environment to be in.

The other way, the way it went, was that we had a great 5 to 6-minute conversation on the product and the company. I was able to explain the history, the culture, and what makes the company & people so special.

We then went our separate directions and they left thinking positively about the company and probably planning their next visit.

When you don't take care of your employees, they won't take care of you and it's the little moments outside of your restaurant that matter just as much as what happens within your restaurant.

Chapter 7:

MAKE EVERY EXPERIENCE PERSONAL

> *"Merely satisfying customers will not be enough to earn their loyalty. Instead, they must experience exceptional service worthy of their repeat business and referral. Understand the factors that drive this customer revolution."*
>
> – Rick Tate

America still uses the tipping system and regardless if you agree with it or not, a personal experience is one of the determining factors whether or not the server will get a good tip from a bad one.

Customers use tips as an incentive for the server to provide an exceptional experience. Some customers even use it as a fear tactic to get what they want but that's not as common as people would like to assume. Out of my 10+ years serving in restaurants, I've only had a handful of these types of customers.

But I used to work the after-bar hours at the only 24-hour restaurant in a town with quite a few bars within walking distance. I worked Thursday-Saturday from 5pm-5:30am so not only did I get to work the dinner rush; I was the only server on the floor for the late-night bar rush.

One night, the overnight cook was coming down with the flu. He had cold sweats, was sniffling, and felt like he was going to pass out so I told him to have a seat since we were usually slow at this time of the year.

About 20 minutes into my nightly cleaning routine, my manager comes over to me and says prepare yourself. He was outside going through his checklist when a caravan of vehicles came pulling into the parking lot.

The restaurant went from a ghost town and turned into the biggest hotspot of the night.

I ran back into the kitchen while everyone was getting situated and asked the cook how he was feeling. He looked miserable and said there was no way that he could cook for a huge rush.

It was just the 3 of us so the manager couldn't run into the back to assist with cooking because he had yet to be trained on the line.

Luckily, leading up to this night, I had been befriended the cooks at the restaurant and they would let me make my own food on overnights (I had an intrigue in becoming a chef at the time).

But there the overnight cook was sitting, basically hurling into a garbage can and there was nobody on-call that would be able to make it in before things got ugly. So, I did what I had to do – make the best out of the situation.

I went into that dining room ready for battle. I was hopping around from table to table taking food orders left and right. Luckily, my manager was getting everyone's drink order to help ease the burden so we were quickly moving through every table.

This was the absolute best situation to be in on overnights though because everyone is still happy from being buzzed (or drunk) and they're still enjoying their time with friends while waiting for their food.

I had an incredibly large table of 15 during this rush and I will always remember this party because they were the ones that asked me to come over to discuss something with them.

Although I could have said that I didn't have time, I took the time to hear them out. Of course, my manager saw this at the time and went around making sure the other tables were being tended to while my attention was being taken up for a short period of time.

The woman that asked me to come over was definitely the life of the party and she asked me how I could maintain such a genuine smile while being the only server in a restaurant packed to capacity.

I looked her square in the eyes and said, "It's my responsibility to ensure you have an amazing time while enjoying your meal. Y'all had fun at the bars and now you're grabbing a bite before heading home for the night so until you're back on the road – you're stuck with me so I don't know who you pissed off but Karma's not in your favor tonight, is it?"

The whole party just started chuckling.

She asked me why I kept running back into the kitchen so many times and I told her that truth is, the cook was under the weather and unable to handle food so I was cooking in addition to serving.

[Let's just say, my hands were shot after having to continuously wash them so many times.]

She looked at me and said, "I like you. Now get me my food before you burn it."

I continued to check in on the tables and as the dining room cleared out, she came over to me and let me know that her experience was the best experience that she had at the restaurant.

Once they left, I went to go close her tab and inside was $250 for a tip with a note that said, "*Thank you for an amazing experience. You didn't show any signs of struggle or overwhelm even with the kitchen situation and you still were able to keep us entertained along with every other table that was in here tonight. We will definitely be back and continue to request your section. You made my night and it has been a rough couple of years so thank you for treating us like we were the only table in the restaurant. Enjoy your tip – you deserve it!"*

It was in that moment that I understood creating unforgettable experiences is what creates loyal customers.

Loyal customers usually make up about 20-25% of your customer base. According to Thanx, the biggest spenders in your restaurant generate about 65% of your revenue*.

The thing is, I didn't just impact the woman who left an amazing tip. I impacted the whole party and they all came in on separate occasions outside of their bi-weekly bar excursions on the weekends.

That's why when I say that customer service is the bottom line, I absolutely mean it. The biggest way to impact your sales within your restaurant instantly is to have a team of people who strive to make someone's life better with every table.

That's why the hiring process is so vital to the success of your restaurant. You cannot train someone to care. You can try but it's going to cost you more in the long run so it's super important to hire right the first time around.

You can spend exorbitant amounts of money in marketing efforts and initiatives but that's only going to attract people into your restaurant. Of course, that's exactly what you want – don't get me wrong but what happens once they step foot in the door?

Having personal experiences is going to take you from a 'one and done' type of restaurant and turn you into the hot spot in your own community. Experiences are absolutely everything – that's why Disney puts so much effort into experience every guest has.

Walt Disney World in Orlando, FL has taken this type of philosophy to the next level.

When you book your trip and you stay at a hotel within the park, they send you a wristband. Each wrist band is personalized to every person on the trip with you. So, when you get to the park, it acts as a communication device throughout the park to create a magical experience.

Kids absolutely love it because as they're leaving a ride or attraction, some places have signs that say "Thank you for riding _____!" and it magically puts their name into the space creating a magical experience for kids and adults.

But this same methodology needs to be implemented within your restaurant in order to continue to retain every customer that walks through the doors.

Restaurant owners & operators focus so much on outreach and attracting new customers that they forget to put focus into their service. The only way to retain customers and get them coming back in is by creating unforgettable experiences within your restaurant. Period.

Chapter 8:

HOW CAN YOU BUILD AN EXCEPTIONAL, CUSTOMER-CENTRIC TEAM?

> *"Employees will go the extra mile for a company if they know the company cares about them. The opposite is also true."*
>
> – Shep Hyken

The trick to building an exceptional, customer-centric team is to constantly be looking for top talent. There should never be a time when your restaurant isn't at least actively looking for exceptional people to join your team because the truth is, not everyone is going to stick around forever – nor do you want them to.

The longer someone is at a job, the more comfortable they tend to get and it's important that companies with high standards continue to uphold those standards to everyone on the team so they don't get complacent.

You want your team to be challenged every single day and to feel like they are making an impact within the company instead of feeling like a warm body that does the job and goes home.

It's time to shift your mindset away from always being reactive when it comes to your restaurant. You want to be able to analyze everything and be able to make decisions that benefit the company instead of making decisions out of instant necessity because that's not always going to be the most beneficial process during times of high stress.

Once you get the right people into your business, then the next step is to get them into your training program.

The biggest issue with the majority of restaurant training is that they are simply being used to get someone on the schedule. But isn't that the main reason to train a new employee anyway? To get them on the schedule and get them proficient enough so they don't need a trainer watching them & eating up labor?

Yes, and no.

You need to start looking at your training program as a paid stage or a qualification process instead of the means to train someone to get on the schedule.

Remember, if you want to be the best in the eyes of the customers, you also have to be the best in the eyes of your employees as well. Which means that your standards matter and they need to be taken seriously.

The restaurant industry has always struggled with high turnover and the people who are hopping from job to job tend to not take training seriously. I mean, let's be honest, once you've served at a restaurant, you could technically serve at any other restaurant.

But that doesn't mean that they have an understanding of your culture or the techniques that you use in your restaurant. Unfortunately, most employees don't understand that because they see all serving jobs to be the same.

It's your responsibility as the employer to change the game on them. To create a training program that is all about whether or not they're good enough to work in your restaurant. You need to set the standards and expect them to come up or to get cut.

It's really that simple.

But creating an exceptional training program isn't something that can happen overnight. It's a process that is constantly needing to be tweaked and improved every time you train someone new.

Successful companies utilize this methodology when it comes to training because they understand the difficulty of finding quality people. When you create an experience that is unlike any others and make the employees fight for their seat at the table, you will be able to find the needle in the haystack.

What If You Don't Have a Training Program?

Create one – immediately. If you don't have one and don't have the time to create one, you need to hire outside help to help you craft your training program because it's absolutely vital for the success of your business.

According to Hot Schedules, 25% of employees leave their job because of poor on-boarding or lack of training opportunities within the company their working for.

No one wants to be stuck at a dead-end job and the quickest way to prove that you aren't a growing company is to not have these systems in place. Training is the single most important piece of the restaurant puzzle.

You cannot create exceptional experiences or improve your bottom line without knowledgeable staff.

By not having a training program, you are telling your employees that you aren't taking this seriously so why should they take the job seriously?

If you don't have a training program or don't have manuals – it's time to put in the effort to create them.

What Your Training Program Should Consist of...

Your training program needs to be able to take someone from just some random person into a brand enthusiast. Chili's turns people from someone who has heard about Chili's into a Chili-Head!

That's exactly what you want your training program to do at your restaurant and don't accept anything less!

Your training program needs to teach new employees the culture & value systems in order to instill pride & prestige into working at your establishment. With that pride and prestige comes career growth and development.

That's the gist of every successful training program.

It's a necessity to treat your training program as a living thing that continues to grow over time. The biggest issue with continuing to work and improve your training program is that it's easy to overcomplicate everything.

Dom Perry said the thing that makes Chili's training program so successful from is that they never forget the basics. That's crucial to understand because we're in a technology-driven society where we are always trying to figure out how to be more innovative with everything that we do.

The first step in creating an exceptional training program is to never get away from the basics.

The next thing to realize is that your training is the foundation to everything that happens within your restaurant.

81

Without a solid foundation, things will slip through the cracks. With a strong foundation, you will be able to focus more on initiatives to grow the restaurant instead of fixing problems and being reactionary in your own business.

An exceptional training program will not only teach the employee everything that they need to know to be successful in their job duties, but it provides them with enough life skills where they could turn around and be a leader within the industry – no matter where they ended up working next.

You probably have a confused look on your face. You read that right. You want your training program to better every employee that comes through your business.

Jim Sullivan sums it up with this quote from the book *Service that Sells*:

"What if I spend the time, money, and effort to train team members and they leave? What if you don't and they stay?"

Getting a new employee up and running may be expensive to get it right but it will save you more effort and headaches down the road to train them right the first time.

Your goal should be to create more leaders and to train your team to think instead of creating a team of followers who will only do what they are told. That's what frustrates most managers in the industry – they aren't training their team to think!

The second any of the employees have a question, they ask the manager and the manager gives them the answer. That's not doing your business any good because if your employees aren't thinking, they're only going through the motions.

When you empower your employees to think, that's when things start improving as a collective instead of putting all of the responsibility on your shoulders.

A team that thinks will find better and more efficient ways of doing something, will create money saving measures, and even attract more people to your restaurant because they are proud to work for a company that values their thoughts and opinions.

How Does This Translate to Being Customer-Centric?

Let's dive into this because the title of this chapter is how to build an exceptional, customer-centric team and I have yet to directly communicate it.

Your core values for your business needs to be customer focused. When you are a customer focused company, you will do anything to make sure the customer has an exceptional experience.

Every meal that you put on the table, every photo you hang in the restaurant, everything that your staff does – all has to have a deliberate intention to enhance the experience for the customer.

I do not believe that the customer is always right but just because they're wrong at times, doesn't mean that you still shouldn't be focused on the customer's happiness. It also means that you get to improve on your operations because they're going to let you know where you fell short in their eyes.

Don't be upset about any feedback that you receive. You can either choose to ignore it or put it into the files and do something about it.

Regardless, you want to make sure that everything that you do has a reason. If a customer is upset, fix it. They're the ones who pay the bills and allow you to create jobs in the first place. It's important to make every customer feel important. Always.

In terms of training, you want to make sure that your staff is knowledgeable enough to be able to handle any situation in the restaurant. I mean, ANY situation.

With Spiderman, with great power comes great responsibility. This is the same thing when it comes to restaurants. With owning/running a restaurant, comes great responsibility to make an impact on everyone who steps in your doors.

If your staff isn't trained or knowledgeable on the company or the product – then you have let your community & your team down.

You need to be organized within your business to make sure that every team member is fully equipped to handle any situation, to make any situation better, and to understand that providing individual experiences to every customer that walks through those doors – will not only benefit the business but it will benefit everyone within the community.

By not having an effective training program, you are being selfish. It's time to empower everyone in your business to help you grow it to levels you could only dream of.

Tony Robbins always says the difference between successful people and unsuccessful people is the ability to be resourceful.

How can you empower your team to be resourceful once they are fully trained and ready to hit the floor?

Chapter 9:

HOW TO CREATE A TRAINING PROGRAM THAT THRIVES!

> *"The secret of change is to focus all of your energy, not on fighting the old, but on building the new."*
>
> - Socrates

When we were opening a restaurant in the Orange County area, I was working closely with our Director of Operations. We finished up a morning training session on day one when he pulls the training team to the side.

He looked at us and mentioned what we were doing right. He loved the energy that we were bringing and loved the content but we were already creating bad habits. I looked confused so he told a story about when he opened up a new store for The Counter Burger.

He was teaching the kitchen on how to properly cut certain cuts of meat. He trained them on what NOT to do first, and then showed them the proper way to cut the meat. He finished the training, got the store opened, and then checked back in 30 days later.

He walked back to the kitchen on day 30 and saw that everyone was doing exactly what he told them NOT to do. Confused, he asked why they were cutting them that way. The kitchen said that that's the way that he showed them how to do it.

It took him twice as long to get them out of those bad habits than it did to train them on how to do something.

So when he told us that story, he said that we were spending half of our time telling our trainees what NOT to do instead of focusing on what they SHOULD be doing every single time.

It was in that moment that I finally understood the importance of creating an effective training program.

When I was 21 years old, I started falling in love with human psychology and how we communicate to people. I ended up finding a company called Transform Destiny that taught NLP (Neuro Linguistic Programming). I studied the power of language and how we can influence people based off of the words we say and how we say them.

Which is the reason why I fell in love with training and am a huge advocate of training programs because your training program sets the tone for your company. It is the foundation that will either allow you to continue building up and thriving or will show the cracks and you'll have to repair that foundation before you can build higher.

According to HotSchedules, 25% of employees will leave their job because of poor on-boarding or lack of training opportunities within your restaurant. That's a quarter of the people that you hire and shows how important your training program is.

So how can you create an effective training program? It starts with having an understanding of what your training program is supposed to look like.

Your training program MUST be able to take someone with zero to little experience and turn them into a professional.

Most companies believe that a training program is a linear thing that they need to check off of the list when they are growing their business. It's not just a box that needs to be checked – it's a box that needs to be checked on a daily, weekly, monthly, quarterly, and yearly basis!

There's a reason why it's called training & development!

Development doesn't just happen over a short period of time. You have to be willing to put in the effort to invest in your employees and it only just starts with your training program.

If you currently don't have a training program in place, then this is the chapter for you. If you already have a training program in place but looking to enhance it, skip over to the next chapter.

I would advise to continue reading to see how you can improve your training structure before skipping this chapter but I'm always looking for ways to improve. Even if I think I already know something, that doesn't mean that I won't learn something by hearing or reading something I believe I already know. I may find that nugget that I was looking for to take everything to the next level.

You're probably thinking to yourself, what does customer service have to do with your training program? It has EVERYTHING to do with it because if your team has a firm understanding of their position and the company, they're able to make decisions to ensure the customer leaves satisfied. Culture trickles down, not upwards.

So let's get into it.

The first thing that we need to do is shift our thinking about what training actually means. Your training program needs to have a goal and the most effective training programs have this one goal in mind: Does this person have what it takes to work for this company?

Most companies think of their training program as a program to get them onto the schedule but if you want longevity & sustainability in this industry – you need to be looking further than your competitors.

You set the standards. It's the person's responsibility to either measure up to those standards or find a different job with another company. You cannot compromise your standards because you're desperate to get warm bodies in your restaurant. That will do more harm than good. So if you can answer "yes" to the question, "Does this person have the willingness and capabilities to reach our standards and execute them on a daily basis?" – throughout ALL of the training – then they qualified to move onto the schedule.

The second thing that you need to do is to list out all of the positions that you currently have within your restaurant. Do you currently have a job description for each position or are you just putting "server" up on the job board and hoping that people have an understanding of what YOUR expectations are of a server?

Like I've said in past chapters, this is your restaurant. This is your baby. You are the one with a vision and an understanding of what you want your culture to be. Once you have a firm understanding of your vision and culture, then you get to form your expectations of every job within your restaurant.

The third thing that you need to do is to create a training manual that walks you through all of the necessary information to do each job properly.

Your training manuals should be so detailed that they could take the training manual home, read it, and be able to come back to your restaurant and begin work on DOING the job.

There are 2 elements to your training manuals that I have learned while creating training manuals that started from blank documents.

1. Infuse your training manual with your culture. There's nothing worse than a stale training manual that puts you to sleep. When you infuse your culture into your training manuals, your employees will begin to have a deeper connection and understanding of WHO you are as a company from day ONE.

2. The other element and why it's necessary to have a training manual is because everyone learns differently. Some people learn by doing, some people learn by listening, and some people learn by reading. This training manual allows the people who learn through reading the ability to retain information that they learned on the job quicker than they would by all hands-on learning.

Your training manuals should be a step-by-step read through of how to do the job. Like we talked about earlier in this chapter, you should always focus on the positives of your expectations – what one must "always do" in this position instead of focusing on the "what not's" of the position.

Once you get the basic learnings down in your training manuals, go back through it and infuse your culture throughout it. Since it's a step-by-step walk-through of the position, it should be read as something conversational.

This enables the human mind to retain more of what they learned on a daily basis. HotSchedules also released that most new hires forget about 70 percent of what is taught within 24 hours of the training experience so if they can walk away with a manual that sounds just like their trainer – they'll be able to retain more and at a faster pace.

Section Recap:

1. Training is meant to see if they have what it takes to work at your restaurant.

2. Create an outline/job description of every position that include your standards, values, and expectations.

3. Create training manuals for every position within your restaurant – this includes hard skills to do the actual position as well as soft skills needed to fulfill the understanding of every position.

If you don't know where to start in terms of creating a training manual – try this exercise.

Exercise: Train someone into a position and record yourself training every day. Once they're fully trained – send the recording to a transcriber. If you cannot afford one, you'll be the transcriber. They will send it to you and you have your foundation of your training manual. Then you will just have to add structure and photos that go with each step of the training.

Training is Meant to be a System

Your training program is supposed to be a system within your restaurant. It's created by you to ensure that your employees will do their job based off of the culture you've created. It sets expectations and allows you to flip on the switch to set the system in motion.

Which is why so many people lean towards opening up franchises because these systems are already created. They are tried and true methods that have worked and continue to work. People who start up new restaurants have an understanding that they must create this system, test it, and continue to refine it.

According to franchise.org, almost three-quarters of the 80 million Millennials in the U.S. say that they want to be entrepreneurs and most of them are perfect candidates for buying franchises.

Why is it that they're looking at franchises instead of starting their own businesses? It's because Millennials look at lifestyle as their #1 determining factor when it comes to being an entrepreneur.

The franchise "plug & play" model allows them to be an entrepreneur with a tried and true method that can potentially get them a quicker return on their investment than they would if they had to create their own systems.

But since you are creating your own training program, you must understand that there will be a learning curve. There will be things that get missed on your first 100 training sessions, which is why it's important to always be evaluating your program after every time you train someone and find ways to improve based on the holes are being displayed by your current staff.

Treat your training manuals as a part of the system. Who is your current head trainer? Is it you? Is it your store manager? Is it your general manager if you have more than one location? Who is in charge of your training?

You cannot let one person be the sole proprietor of the information for that position or for the company. If someone came up to you and asked if they could begin franchising your model – would you be able to hand them over an operations manual and say "here's everything you need to know".

If you cannot confidently say that, then you need to get to work on your training materials. Chances are, your chef trains the BOH team and your manager will train your FOH team. But if your chef or manager got hit by a truck and died – would your system continue to work?

If the answer is no, then you have a lot of work ahead of you. If the answer is yes, then you have a system in place that allows your business to move forward.

I understand that it's not fun to think the head of your team would be killed in a freak accident but as a business owner, your #1 asset is your business and you need to protect your business, first.

You protect the business by getting all of your training materials and programs into place.

Which brings me to the understanding of what makes the system work.

Train the trainer

The purpose of train the trainer is to turn someone from an inexperienced trainer into a competent trainer for the company.

Again, this needs to be written down into a manual but the beauty of train the trainer is that your training manuals that you created for each position should be created as the train the trainer materials as well.

So if your head trainer gets hit by a truck and misses his training day, someone else can grab the training materials and be able to train someone – even if they haven't trained someone before.

Why would you want someone training someone that hasn't been trained on training someone properly? You don't! But you need to have your systems in place for worst-case scenarios. Always protect your business, first.

But when you begin to implement the train the trainer model in your restaurant, you will never have to rely solely on one person in the business and will be able to constantly be improving your operations – no matter what day, time, or shift it is.

Trainers should also know the different learning styles and have the ability to figure out a learning style instantly by the first time they step onto the floor.

Learn to Adapt to Different Learning Styles

New employees love organization and having these training manuals will show them that you're serious about your company and the position they're agreeing to work at. But what's going to set you apart is to learn HOW to train your employees within your training program.

As a trainer, it's your responsibility to be able to understand the learning styles. Why does it matter? Shouldn't someone just be able to listen, do it, and then I get to go back to focusing on getting more customers into the restaurant? Sure, but if you don't set your team up for success, your business will fail.

When you understand learning styles, you will be able to train people quicker and get them to retain more so you shorten the length of time of your training program and can put more effort into excellence.

What are the different learning styles?

This is where my love for NLP comes into play and why I believe that everyone should have an understanding of the human mind. There are 4 different learning styles that are crucial to integrate with your training.

1. Visual
2. Auditory
3. Kinesthetic
4. Auditory Digital

Let's dive a little deeper into what these words even mean and how you can add these layers into your training program.

Visual

People who are visual learners usually memorize by seeing pictures and are less distracted by noise. They often have trouble remembering and are bored by long verbal instructions as their mind may wander. They are interested in how things LOOK.

Visual learners learn by seeing how it's done, which is why having photos in your manuals are critical in hitting all learning styles. You will also notice that when you are showing someone on how to do a certain objective or training up a certain skill (ex: carrying 3 plates at once), they will be WATCHING what you are doing instead of looking at you while you're talking.

Don't get offended by that because they are learning based off of what THEY know works best for them. When you notice that you have a lot of visual learners on the team you're training, take the time to SHOW them all of the steps to ensure they can complete each exercise/task.

Auditory

Auditory learners are usually distracted by a lot of noise or side conversations. They can repeat things back to you easily and will learn by LISTENING to the words that are coming out of your mouth.

They will be the ones that will learn more from reading the manual out loud than from actually watching or doing the task at hand. They are also very sensitive to the tone of the trainer as well as why it's important to put vocal emphasis on things that are important.

Your trainers set the tone. When you infuse your culture into your training program, your trainer is the ambassador of your restaurant. They need to understand that they will have auditory learners and should understand the importance of tone, emphasis, and communication in general.

Kinesthetic

Kinesthetic people learn by DOING something or getting walked through it on a step-by-step basis. But they are very hands on so there's no point in telling them HOW to do something without letting them dive in and simply do the activity.

New hires that are kinesthetic learners will tend to get distracted when you are showing them or making them listen to you while you explain the task at hand.

An effective trainer will be able to utilize this person as their demo person to show the rest of the group how to do something so that way, the kinesthetic learner will get to learn while you teach the rest of the group based off of their own learning styles.

Auditory Digital

Last but not least, the auditory digital learners are people who will memorize steps, procedures, and sequences of events which is why I have mentioned training manuals MUST have step-by-step processes within them.

They want to have a full understanding of the whole process before it "makes sense" to them. I could show someone how to hold 3 plates at once but they would be a visual learner. The auditory digital learner will need to hear, see, and understand the step by step process of HOW to hold each plate to achieve the action of holding 3 plates at once.

Now that you have an understanding of the different types of learning styles that your new hires will have, how do you integrate all of this information into your training program?

Let's talk about the host position within a restaurant. How do you train a host for your restaurant by utilizing ALL of these learning styles?

1. Write the objective of the position
2. Create the training program based around the host position

3. Create a step-by-step process for every activity you need the host to do

4. Create an exercise that gets the new hire up and doing the activity

5. After they do the activity, use coaching techniques to improve how they can get better – continue building upon the foundation and improving their skills

Now, you're probably thinking that if you were to sit down and write an in-depth training manual for every position with step-by-step processes of everything, that the training manual would be so many pages. Well, the truth is, yes it will. That's what you need to ensure that your manuals are a system.

You are building a system that works and it shouldn't matter WHO you plug into that system, it should run based on the settings that you created. If your manager trains someone, they should be saying the exact same thing in the exact same way as the owner does. That's why systems work.

Once all is said and done, you should have a physical sign off that the employee has an understanding of every aspect of the expectations and duties of the position. That way, if they ever say that they weren't trained on something but signed off on it, you will be able to hold them accountable. We'll talk about that more later on in the book.

How Can You Enhance Your Training Program?

Once you have your core training program in place, you need to have additional opportunities for development to grow through the position and have upward mobility. Even if you currently don't have a position available, you need to have a mentoring system in place to retain your employees.

Here are some ways to enhance your training program and continue to develop your employees on a daily basis.

1. On-Demand Learning

The one thing that employees are seeking is the ability to improve their skills on their time. That's why digital products are HOT in the internet marketing industry and courses are something to consider.

People who are seeking higher learning will be given the ability to login on their time and develop their skills – when they want to. In the age of social media and having a social presence, people are always looking at how to show off in their life.

When someone takes the time to develop their skills or understanding of the skills they're learning, they are the ones who are always seeking another promotion. They are looking for growth which is why having an on-demand learning portal will always be a win-win for your restaurant.

Especially since attention spans are getting shorter and shorter, your ability to create engaging trainings on important aspects of your business will help create more leaders in this industry as well as set your restaurant up for massive success within your community.

People who are proud of where they work will be more excited to tell their friends to visit them during work or to recommend your restaurant for people who are coming into town. When they take pride in where they work, they begin to feel a sense of ownership and will do whatever it takes to succeed.

Having employees with a sense of ownership is the end goal. When they have a sense of ownership, they will always go above and beyond every single day. No matter what.

By having an on-demand learning portal, you are able to create unique learning opportunities. Quizzes and tests are no longer formal tests and gets rid of that anxiety people have surrounding the word "test". Turn it into a game and see which employee can get the highest score. Gamify your on-going training & development!

2. Results Orientated Metrics

Another way to enhance your training program is to ensure you have solid metrics in place to be able to measure the training and development of your team. If you have someone that's interested in managing a team but have zero experience, how are they supposed to show you a metric that they have what it takes to step up without you taking the full risk?

Set short-term, obtainable goals that allow you to test them throughout their shifts. Also, have them show you how they are taking the initiative to learn about leadership outside of the hours they are working within your restaurant's walls.

A leader is constantly looking to learn, grow, and improve. If they are reading books on leadership or management – this is a great quality to see that they are ready.

When you create a leadership style culture that focuses on learning & development inside of the company, they will also look outside of the company to develop their skills.

3. Create a Training University

At the end of the day, there is no "one size fits all" training solution. You are constantly having to find new ways to teach people and there is so much technology that is affordable where you can implement this enhancement quicker than you realize.

I'm not talking about putting your whole training program into a video learning library but the KEY points that you see people constantly struggle with or something that takes a long time to learn – put that information into a video library.

This works great with bartenders. If you have a specific way of mixing cocktails and want them to learn how to make your ever-changing cocktail list – what a better way to get them to learn the drink than showing them BEFORE their next shift!

There are programs out there that allow you to rollout a short video on the new cocktail, the ingredients, how to make it, and then when they come into their next shift – they must show the manager that they are able to make it.

People are perfectionists and want to do things right the first time. Which is why training & development is crucial to your success as a thriving restaurant.

Of course, not everyone that works in your restaurant is going to want to be developed. Some are simply there for a paycheck and have a life outside of your restaurant. That's perfectly fine. But while they're clocked-in, it's imperative to set up a culture of ownership while they're working.

But having access to development is going to show your team that you care about them on another level and will give them a buy in that they will not get at other restaurants.

When I was growing up in the restaurant industry, there wasn't a development process. I wasn't the best sales person either because I didn't care about numbers as a server. I just got disciplined for not hitting certain sales goals.

So I was frustrated when I would get written up over something silly and the manager or company wouldn't take the time to explain to me HOW to hit the sales goals. I ended up quitting that job because I was still new to the world of serving at that time.

But I got another job as a server and the manager pulled me aside to figure out why I didn't hit my sales goals for the week. After learning that I wasn't a great sales person, he gave me some tactics on how he used to hit the sales goals. He gave me a step-by-step process and if I followed the tactics, that I would win.

The following week, I implemented his tools & tactics. I was skeptical but I wanted higher tips and he said that I would probably get tipped higher with a larger guest check average.

Low and behold, at the end of the sales contest, I was further ahead than anyone else because I had a manager that cared. Your systems will work when your key hires are exceptional at their job and you must either find exceptional people or develop your team to be exceptional.

Which is why the goal of a training program should be to come up to your standards instead of just getting on the schedule. You will automatically weed out the people who don't care and your restaurant will be the place all of your customers want to come to because the employees enjoy their time working there.

That's what it boils down to and why your training program is so important.

At the end of the day, customer service IS the bottom line. You cannot increase your revenue without having exceptional people. You cannot have exceptional people if you do not focus on developing the people that you do have.

Your frontline people are the ones who can make or break your restaurant. They are the ones that need to have an understanding of the importance of your mission. They are the ones who are going to bat for you on a daily basis, every time that they clock-in to their shift.

They are the ones who will setup the experience that your restaurant is going for. The experience the customer has is going to be the lasting experience that they will leave with. Your frontline people are the ones who will either get the customer to come back or will prevent the customer from returning to your restaurant.

The experience rests on the shoulders of the people in charge of your customer service.

If you want to grow your bottom line, start by developing your people.

Chapter 10:

EFFECTIVE TRAINING MEANS HOLDING YOUR TEAM ACCOUNTABLE

"You have to hold people accountable. You're not always going to be the most popular. If you want to win, sometimes you have to have a difficult conversation with people. You know they are not going to like you. But you do it because you want what is best for the team."

- Carla Overbeck, Former U.S. Women's Soccer National Team Captain

Why do I talk so much about training? Because it's the one thing in your business that will be able to separate you from everyone else. You get to create a team based off of your values and understanding of what true hospitality is.

Someone can have the exact same concept and build their restaurant to look like yours but the biggest thing that separates you from them is your values and your understanding of those values.

The biggest lesson that I learned while working at The Pie Hole in Los Angeles was learning to hold people accountable.

When I was managing the restaurant, I wasn't holding people accountable. I thought that I was holding people accountable but then when it came to checking over their work for switch over, nothing was getting done. We were running out of things that we shouldn't have and then I would REACT to fix everything.

Then they sat me down and said that I needed to start holding people accountable even more.

The trick is that you cannot hold someone accountable for something that they don't know about.

Which is why we decided it was best to create a robust training program to ensure that nobody within the company could say that they didn't know anything about the operations of the company.

Once they're understanding and officially certified to be on the floor without supervision, that's when holding people accountable comes in.

Now, I've heard a lot that leadership is lonely at the top. I don't believe that's true for a minute because leadership is only lonely when you don't have anybody to relate to. Find people with similar mindsets in similar or higher positions to learn from them and celebrate your successes with.

Jim Rohn always says that you are the sum of the 5 people you hang around the most. So, if YOU are the sum of the 5 people you hang around most, think about it in terms of a leader.

Your team is the sum of the 5 people that they hang around the most – you and your other team members.

In order for your team to be great – you as the leader, must also be great.

In order to have an exceptional team, you have to hold people accountable for not doing their job effectively. Otherwise, you will end up like I was – tired, frustrated, and not an effective leader.

When your team doesn't perform, that's a reflection of you as the leader. So, it's vital to hold people accountable because your team is a reflection of how well you are leading. Which might be a sore eye opener for some but like I said in the previous chapters, leadership is all about self-reflection.

What it boils down to is that you need to do what's absolutely necessary for your team to win because then, the business will win. Your employees will respect you because you are putting the needs of the team ahead of the needs of the individual.

They will take notice and they will back your decisions, every single time. (I know this from experience, myself.)

Hold your teams accountable in order to have them thrive.

Remember, you're the BEST so you always expect the best. If your team doesn't exceed your expectations, then that's a reflection of you – not them.

Lead them.

*   *   *

Let's just be honest with each other for a second. When I was managing restaurants, I learned the hard way why holding people accountable was a necessity. It's not because I'm a horrible person, it's because my job title was to uphold the standards.

As a manager, it's your job to touch every aspect of the restaurant, every single day. You have to assess everything and every little detail. Walking into a restaurant, you see everything as an equation.

You notice when tables seem upset. You notice when your team doesn't look as presentable as they've agreed to per the uniform policy that they signed off on. You notice when something isn't clean or when something breaks.

It's not the most popular job but your sole position is to ensure that the restaurant is profitable and that the operations are running smoothly. Part of the operations is your team.

You are responsible for every decision and choice that they make. (*If you don't agree with me, refer back to Chapter 4.*)

In truth, your team should behave how they are lead. So, if they have an understanding of COGs, an understanding of why they should be guest-centric, an understanding that everything costs money – then they'll have more skin in the game. They'll feel a sense of ownership and step up their own game.

It's all about respect. Respect is earned so in order to receive respect; you must act like someone that deserves respect.

A leader who is respected holds their team accountable because effective leaders don't put up with a mediocre team that only cares some times. When someone breaks standards, they must be held accountable. Period.

That's how you strengthen your team. The conversation of the reason WHY you are holding them accountable is where the respect will be earned.

Chapter 11:

THE MISSING ELEMENT IN THE MAJORITY OF RESTAURANTS IS...

> *"A coach is someone who tells you what you don't want to hear, who has you see what you don't want to see, so you can be who you always knew you could be."*
>
> – Tom Landry

The missing element that most restaurants are needing is to have on-going coaching sessions every single day.

I went to Mendocino Farms' Leadership Retreat where all of their newly hired managers or newly promoted managers would go to get a more in depth training on the philosophy of leading.

Mario Del Pero is an exceptional leader. He studies exceptional leaders.

Mario is a big sports fan and he has a sports analogy for everything. But the biggest lesson that I learned from him and his operations is that the managers MUST have a daily check-in with themselves to create a game plan for their shift.

They weren't just coming into their shift and reacting to the issues within the restaurant. They were to walk into their store, take time to self-reflect on what they want to focus on (based on the values & needs of their specific store), and create a game plan to "win the shift".

This was brilliant because I got to watch every manager in that room think about how they could get their team to win the shift. How they could create that one additional meaningful interaction with a customer that could change their life.

The last thing that they would always write down is how they could influence their team to be better than they were the day before.

You need to have thinkers and leaders within your restaurant if you want it to be successful. Surround yourself around the people who want to better and grow the restaurant, not just continue to hit the status quo.

Every shift, you would watch how the managers would be aware of all of their surroundings inside of the restaurant. They notice when a customer isn't satisfied and handle the situation.

At the same time, they are watching every employee interact with the guests and LISTENING to what's being said. If they catch anything, they write it down on their action plan for the shift.

Then they have on-going coaching sessions with their team throughout the shift.

It's that extra layer of accountability that the leaders of the company are always striving for excellence, with everything that they do. The excellence will then trickle down to every employee and create a positive influence that they will then take with them in life. It may not seem like a big deal but on-going coaching is the one thing that can take an ordinary employee and turn them into an exceptional one.

Exceptional isn't achieved by living in a world of mediocrity. Bust through mediocrity by building a team that continues to focus on excellence by providing daily support.

Chapter 12:

WHY YOU NEED A SECRET SHOPPING PROGRAM

> *"The goal as a company is to have customer service that is not just the best but legendary."*
>
> – Sam Walton

In sales, success lies within the follow-up. You need to understand that just because you have an exceptional training program in place doesn't mean that your team will always be the best. Just because you are holding your teams accountable, doesn't always mean they will always be the best.

In order to succeed in the eyes of the customer, you must ALWAYS be following up with how your team is doing.

Whether that's a weekly, monthly, quarterly, or even yearly basis – having a secret shopper program will ensure that your team strives to be the best every single day.

The first thing that we need to get out of the way is that secret shopping programs are NOT just for corporate restaurants. Single-unit, family-owned restaurants need to have a secret shopping program just as much as restaurants that are on store 2, 3, and beyond!

They are important because it allows you to track HOW your team is performing when the owner isn't in the store. It allows you to track HOW your management team is performing. It allows you to track HOW your restaurant runs without your presence.

The biggest issue with secret shopping companies is that they hire a random person to go into the restaurant, purchase one item, look at the bathrooms, look outside, and write down their engagement with the employees on a brief questionnaire.

The reason why the people are even going is because they are getting a free meal out of the deal but the majority of them know absolutely NOTHING about the restaurant industry.

That's the biggest downfall with all of the secret shopping companies that are out there.

The other issue is that they charge quite a bit to get the results. But once the restaurant owner is given the results, they get to walk away with the money and you're stuck in information overload. That's not fair.

Restaurants need to start creating their own secret shopping program where they can put more of that investment back into the development into your own staff to improve their performance.

As a restaurant owner, you need to have an understanding of WHY people are performing the way that they are instead of just having one person come by once and get a free meal.

It would be easier to have a family member or close friend of yours go into the restaurant and purchase something, then report back to you with their findings. At least your friends or family members have more of a buy-in and understanding of your restaurant than some random person on the street.

When I was 18 years old, I saw an ad on a job board that said "Secret Shoppers Needed". They wanted me to go into a restaurant, fill out a Google questionnaire, and that I would get $25-$50 with a reimbursement on the meal.

I went in, looked at the bathrooms, looked at the front door, had a short conversation with the server, paid, then left. That was it. There was no buy-in, I entered basic information, and that's all that there is to it because I just didn't care about anything than what I was getting out of it.

That is why I say that it's important to create your own secret shopping program.

But if you simply don't have the time to get a secret shopping program off of the ground, then it's important to vet the companies that you are going to work with.

The secret shoppers that you want to have into your restaurant should have a deep understanding of the restaurant industry. They should understand workflow, how to upsell, menu engineering, be able to create situations that push your team to the limits, and truly care about the reason behind WHY they are there doing the shop.

They must have an eye to be able to look over everything with a fine tooth comb. They should also be able to come at different times throughout the week to get a feel of every shift and multiple servers.

The reason behind that is you don't know what the issue might be. The secret shopper is going in to see if your team is doing everything in their power to raise the guest check average and providing an exceptional experience based on YOUR brand standards.

Not only do they need to know everything listed above, but they also need to know how a restaurant can FIX the problems that were presented. How can the menu be re-engineered for the highest sales? How can the servers interact differently to get the customer to buy ONE more drink? How can the facilities be better? Is the flow of service hindering table turns?

The list is endless. That is why it's crucial to have someone who understands the industry go through your restaurant and then be able to provide tactics on how to improve your operations.

You wouldn't put a random person in charge of your bottom line so why would you put a random person in charge of judging your operations.

Remember, it's expensive to hire a professional but it can cost twice as much when you hire an amateur.

Chapter 13:

THE #1 TRAIT EVERY RESTAURANT PROFESSIONAL NEEDS TO SUCCEED

"You don't have to be great to start, but you have to start to be great."

– Zig Ziglar

In this book, we've discussed the importance of customer service since it directly affects your bottom line. If you want continue to be successful, you must have a plan in place for your 4-walls marketing efforts.

No matter if you are the restaurant owner/operator/manager/chef – the one thing that we can always control is quality.

Quality of the food, quality of the service, quality of the ambiance & atmosphere, and quality of the customer's overall experience.

But a dream without goals is simply a dream because there's nothing to do to put it into action.

In order to create any kind of success in the restaurant world, you have to get started on initiatives that make sense at the time.

But the ONE thing that you need to do for this year and every year moving forward is to always focus on being exceptional. As a company, as a leader, as an employee, as a person, etc. No matter what – you need to focus on being exceptional.

When you focus on being exceptional, everything else is forced to level up or step out of the way and that's exactly what you need right now.

This goes for your team, your customers, your menu, your restaurant – everything.

The restaurant industry is NOT an easy industry to be in. We work long hours, late nights, weekends, and definitely don't get home when we say we will. If you have a significant other who understands this – thank them!

They're the true heroes.

There will be times when you feel like throwing in the towel. There will be times when all you want to do is throw a chair straight through the window. There will be times when you question if all of the difficulties will be worth it in the end.

I'm telling you – it's all worth it.

This industry is unlike any other in the world because we have a direct ability to change lives on the spot. We have the ability to take someone's bad day and turn it into an exceptional day.

We have the ability to witness major life milestones with people.

Restaurants are still places where people go to sign multi-million dollar contracts, make business deals, propose to their loved ones, gather for family events, celebrate birthdays or anniversaries, etc.

The list is endless.

We get to impact people on a daily basis based on the choices that we, as a team, make every single day. There's nothing better than that.

Whenever you feel like it's not worth it anymore, do me a favor. Find the real reason why you started this journey in the first place. What was it that made you come alive? Make sure you hold it tight within you and let that be your reason why you show up every single day.

Make that be the reason why you don't settle for mediocrity.

Make that be the reason why you always strive for excellence.

Make that be the reason why you never give up.

Be exceptional in business and in life.

All I ask is that you care.

What Happens Next?

Creating a training program is time consuming and when you've never put a system in place, then you're going to feel very overwhelmed.

Don't feel overwhelmed. Ask for help. I wouldn't be where I am today without all of the mentors that I have learned from and all of the people in my life that have believed that it was possible.

If you are thinking of creating a training program but don't know where to begin, let's talk! Reach out.

If you are thinking of creating a secret shopping program but don't know what one consists of or how to utilize the results you get – reach out!

If you are ready to take your business to the next level by implementing what's necessary TODAY for a better TOMORROW ... reach out!

People are always afraid to ask for help but it's better to ask for help NOW to create a solid foundation instead of when everything is falling apart around you. That's when it's probably too late.

Put the right tools and people in place now so you can focus on what matters most – keeping your business open.

You are not alone.

If you have any questions, comments, or concerns – please don't hesitate to reach out. Just head to my website, click on the contact page, and fill it out so we can begin the conversation.

We're all in this industry to share a part of us. Don't let your pride or ego stand in the way of getting the help that you need.

When you're ready to take your restaurant and team to the next level – reach out.

I can't wait to hear from you!

*"Do You Care **Enough**?*
*Do you care **enough** to stand up for something?*
*Do you care **enough** to give it a try, even though it might not work?*
*Do you care **enough** to seek making change in the world?*
*Do you care **enough** to matter?*
*Maybe it's time to find something worth caring **enough** about.*
Otherwise... what's the point?
We get one life. Make it matter."

Chef Chris Hill

FINAL NOTE

Growing up, I have always been one that took risks. I moved away from home with only $1,000 in my pocket when I was 18. I failed. I ended up sleeping on a bench in Los Angeles and terrified to admit defeat.

I ended up moving back home and trying again when I was 20 years old, in 2011. I ended up meeting people that would help shape my life and push me to reach higher than I thought I would ever be able to.

I was never one to let fear stand in my way, ever. I would push forward and lived the life that I wanted to live – until life decided to knock me on my feet. I ended up spending 3 years of my life in and out of the hospital, dealt with heart disease, and living within the confines of my own fear.

I lost myself. I lost myself and the person who I thought I wanted to be. My dreams shifted, my desires shifted, and my values shifted.

It took me 3 years to break free of the jail that I put myself in all because I let fear get the best of me. The only thing that got me through was the restaurant industry because the restaurant has been the only place where I've felt at home.

When you walk into a restaurant, you get to see a piece of someone's life that you'd never thought even existed. You see, restaurants transport you into places you never knew you wanted to be in but once you're in, it wraps its arms around you and holds you tight.

It's the love that someone put into something to share that piece of them with YOU.

If you want to grow in this industry, you have to find that restaurant that understands this and wants to bring you into their family. Although restaurants support over 14 million jobs, the industry is incredibly tight-knit and it's so important to always leave on good terms.

But when you find that restaurant that wants to aide in your growth and development, you want to make sure to learn as much as you possibly can from them. But don't just put all of your eggs in that basket for your own development.

Grow outside of the restaurant so you can bring something valuable into the restaurant which will set you apart from everyone else. It will allow you to put yourself into a leadership position in the company.

Why? Shouldn't a business invest in your training & development? Yes – 100% but it shouldn't stop there because opportunity never rests. It's your job as an employee of a restaurant to create your own opportunities and grow into positions.

As a business owner, you shouldn't just assume your team doesn't want to grow and develop. You should always be looking at ways to train, develop, and invest in your teams. If you currently don't have the capabilities, guide them on where they can go.

That's why I am so proud of where I am because I didn't sit around waiting for opportunities to fall into my lap. I hustled. I worked long hours. I felt drained and like I wanted to quit. I hit that breaking point and didn't think that I had anything left in me to give.

But when I found out who I was and how I wanted to impact the community – I was able to find inspiration and motivation to push forward. To come back into work feeling refreshed and revitalized, even when I was ready to walk away.

It was the belief that my opinion mattered that made me take the risks and put myself out there to spark change.

I owe a lot of my knowledge to The Pie Hole LA. Yes, I have sought after knowledge outside of them BUT I have been able to come back and put my new found knowledge to the test. I found out what was working and if something didn't work, I would ask them how we could make it better. Lindsay, Matt, & Sean have all impacted my life in one way or the other.

Like I said, I was never one to run away from fear. I would always fight through it and The Pie Hole was there during many growth moments of my life. I've made many mistakes but they've never let me feel like I have failed – it was always a teaching moment.

That's why it is SO important to put more focus on your training & development because this industry and this world needs more leaders. They need people who will continue to persevere through the darkest of times and come out stronger on the other side.

As people, we are all fighting battles in our lives because life is a rollercoaster. There are times when you win and there are times when you learn but always strive to be better today than you were yesterday.

So I wanted to publicly acknowledge how much of an impact that their company had on my growth and development. I found myself within their company and will never forget it.

Made in the USA
Columbia, SC
29 June 2018